Praise for Beth Lisick's Everybody into the Pool

"I can't remember the last time I had this much fun reading. Crazy life, crazy times, crazy San Francisco culture, yes, but we never lose track of that cheerful suburban squirrel of a girl from the family in which the dad circulates memos to his children announcing Family Night. I loved it.

—Tamim Ansary, author of
West of Kabul, East of New York

"Beth Lisick's voice is crackling, super-energized; her eye for irony, comedy and truth sweeps through pop culture's absurd terrain and lands right in her own pocket—no one escapes her brutal honesty, not even her own terrific self."

—Michelle Tea, author of
Valencia and *The Chelsea Whistle*

"Lisick's wickedly sharp, poetically ironic, a captivating storyteller, always fresh, and super-entertaining."

—Po Bronson, author of
What Should I Do with My Life?

"Lisick makes me laugh, laugh, laugh. Her essays are funny, smart, and sharp. She dives into the world of America's subcultures, a wolf in girl-next-door's clothing, and comes out with something even a grandmother could love."

—James Frey, author of
A Million Little Pieces

EVERYBODY INTO THE POOL

TRUE TALES

BETH LISICK

10 ReganBooks
Celebrating Ten Bestselling Years
An Imprint of HarperCollins*Publishers*

I write about my family, my husband, and my husband's family in this book. I use their real names with their blessings, more or less. There are a few names I chose to change because I hate to make anyone feel too uncomfortable.

HarperCollins books may be purchased for educational, business, or sales promotional use. For information please write: Special Markets Department, HarperCollins Publishers Inc., 10 East 53rd Street, New York, NY 10022.

FIRST EDITION

Designed by Kris Tobiassen

All illustrations throughout by David L. Cooper

Printed on acid-free paper

Library of Congress Cataloging-in-Publication Data

Lisick, Beth, 1968–
    Everybody into the pool / Beth Lisick.—1st ed.
        p. cm.
    ISBN 0-06-077877-6 (acid-free paper)
    1. Lisick, Beth, 1968- 2. Authors, American—20th century—Biography. 3. Lisick, Beth, 1968—Homes and haunts—California—San Francisco. 4. San Francisco (Calif.)—Social life and customs. I. Title.

PS3562.I77Z47 2005
818'.5409—dc22
[B]
                                                                    2005042833

05 06 07 08 09 WBC/RRD 10 9 8 7 6 5 4 3 2 1

CONTENTS

FIRST, LET ME EXPLAIN

A few months ago, I was at my parents' house having dinner, and my mom was talking about someone she recently met. "I felt just awful for him," she said, dipping her knife into the I Can't Believe It's Not Butter. "He's the first person I've ever met in my life who was actually *emotionally scarred* by his childhood." I tried really hard not to laugh, but did anyway because I can be a jerk sometimes. "What's so funny?" she said, looking around the table at everybody, slightly bewildered. There was no reaction from my dad who, still in Phase I of the South Beach Diet, was busy searching underneath his skinless chicken breast for a carb. When my mom saw how my older brother Chris fake-coughed and grinned into his lap, she knew something was up. "What?" she pleaded. "I'm not getting the joke." She then looked to Paul, my oldest brother, who is oblivious in most social situations and hadn't heard a word she'd said.

INTRODUCTION

I searched for a gentle way of breaking the news to her: "Mom, practically everybody is traumatized by their childhoods." I felt guilty for springing this on her and corrupting her innocence, but I couldn't help myself. I was experiencing a wave of that same juvenile instinct I had in the early nineties, when I felt compelled to tell her which of her favorite celebrities were gay. Then she got a panicky look on her face, carefully set down her fork with a cherry tomato still speared on it, and said with so much sincerity it nearly broke my heart, "Honey, were you *traumatized* by your childhood?"

Now, the archetype of the emotionally charged familial dinner is one all of us know well. This question would normally mark the trigger point where the kid blows up and unleashes a laundry list of past trespasses, flying off the handle about Lake Tahoe 1978 or Repressed Body Memories, or "I never wanted to play the flute—*you* wanted to play the flute, Dad!" Or else the kid summons up steely resolve and says quietly, "No, Mother, of course not. I was perfectly happy." And then everybody eats the rest of their meal in a silence that would best be described by a foley artist as "independent film, suburban ennui dinner table silence." However, neither of these things happened that night because I lucked out.

I think I was raised in what used to be referred to as a "normal" family back before everybody discovered that most normal families were messed up. We didn't have a dark side. (But for the record, I am a huge fan of anything involving screwed-up, suburban people popping pills and unintenionally harming others with their self-absorption.) I went to church every Sunday, had happily married parents, and walked down the street to my public school. I was an honor student, a track star, and a homecoming princess. It seemed as if I was on my way to becoming a highly functioning member of society or at least someone who wouldn't end up living the way I did. I'm talking about the illegal warehouse spaces, the ten-year lapse without seeing a doctor or dentist, driving cars held together by Bondo, crashing on floors across the United States and Europe while touring with my "poetry." Now, at age thirty-five, my yearly income hovers right near the poverty line.

The weird thing is that I'm pretty sure it was my normal upbringing that did this to me, but not because I was ever rebelling, slumming, or trying to escape the Stepford-pod people. I loved my normal upbringing. I just think the fact that I had a stable childhood was precisely what let me stray pretty far away from it without ever landing in therapy, rehab, or jail or having an identity crisis, eating disorder, drug problem, or prescription for antidepressants. I inherited my parents' sensible, traditional approach to living, which kept me grounded when their Midwestern openmindedness and acceptance got me into a lot of nontraditional situations.

So the stories in this book are about turning out too weird to fit into the mainstream world, the one I came from, but being too normal for the fringe world I found later. I drive a station wagon, just like my mom did, but I live on a block that has two drug dealers who—like neighbors should—know me by name. I like to bake, I make my own chicken stock, and I have slept on the same ratty pillow for twelve years. I'm married, but I don't wear a ring. My wed-

INTRODUCTION

ding ceremony was performed by my gay father-in-law who's married to my lesbian mother-in-law who lives with her female lover. I still hold the long jump record at my high school. I toured with Lollapalooza in exchange for a few sandwiches. I've never borrowed a dime from my parents. I don't have any tattoos. My husband's middle name is Hamburger Hot Dog. The material possession I most desire is a dishwasher. I still perform for beer sometimes. When I'm alone, I sometimes shout, "Okay, people and porpoises!" for no reason. One of my favorite things in the world is toast. I never made out with my girlfriends, but I once had strap-on sex with a lady construction worker named Trouble. I'm not a cat person, a dog person, or even a baby person, but I'm a parent.

So that's me. Probably not too different from you, except with varying haircuts or health care providers or food allergies. I think all of us feel normal and yet not normal. When it's so easy to think of yourself as a big mess in this world, it helps to convince yourself that at least you're a well-adjusted one.

EVERYBODY INTO THE POOL

1
GREETINGS FROM OUR SPECIAL BUBBLE

The fact that my parents moved to Northern California during the fabled "Summer of Love" can be explained this way: In addition to Free Love and War Protests, another hot ticket in the year 1967 was Guided Missiles. The aerospace industry was booming, and my dad, the son of a former coal miner named Cubby, had just become the first person in his family to go to college. He finished his engineering degree in Illinois and decided to move west. While vibrant young people across the nation were making pilgrimages to the Haight Ashbury in San Francisco, my parents found Mecca in Sunnyvale, near the Lockheed Missiles and Space plant and about forty-five minutes away from any genus or species of counterculture movement. If it weren't for public television documentaries and *Life* magazine, they would have never known that there were excessively hairy people getting busy in Golden Gate Park, shaking ribbon-festooned tambourines in one hand and holding doobies in the other. As my mom sums it up, "With two boys under two and you on the way, we were pretty darn busy ourselves."

Fast forward to one Thursday evening in the fall of 1972. It's been a big year so far. Vietnam is out of control, Watergate is heating up, and my parents sit the three of us down on the couch to alert us to an important event that will change our lives. From now on, every Thursday night will hereby be known as Family Night. My mom explains that Family Night will be a special evening when we can look forward to "relaxing" and "enjoying one another's company"—concepts difficult for pre-elementary school age children to latch onto until my dad clarifies matters for us: "That means no TV."

It seemed impossible to imagine it. Our TV was like the household sundial, always there to give us a rough estimate of the time. *Lilias, Yoga and You* meant it was still too early to wake Mom up. Nap time was in sync with *As the World Turns*. Dinner ended just before Walter Cronkite came on. Ignoring the panic on our young faces, Dad presented us with a typed agenda. Even at ages four, five, and six, my brothers and I knew there was something odd about your dad handing you a memo. We had long harbored a vague suspicion that he thought of us as his employees, and the itemized schedule was a disturbing development.

As two people who spent the 1940s and 1950s growing up in working class Catholic families in small-town Illinois, my parents were about as wholesome and earnest as twin ears of corn at a church picnic. They were naïve, sweet, and open to just about anything—as long as it wasn't illegal or didn't hurt anyone's feelings. It's so easy to picture my mom reading about Family Night in *Redbook, Ladies Home Journal,* or one of those confusing mom magazines that features pictures of roasted meats and patio furniture. The little thought bubble over her head would say, "What a fun idea!" and that's exactly what would come out of her mouth.

Some people get criticized for saying whatever pops into their heads because their heads are full of darkness, sarcasm, and brutal truths. With my mom, it's the opposite. Her world is full of neat people! Interesting places! Fun ideas! And she's not afraid to let her little light shine. Irony, for her, was what she had to do with all those clothes in the basket over there, and jaded was a pretty, green Oriental stone. And she knew about the Orientals because her high school football team had been called the Pekin Chinks. Their mascot was a toothy, slanty-eyed guy wearing a coolie hat until sometime in the mid-seventies when, under advisement, they became the Dragons. Everyone in town felt just awful about the misunderstanding. They'd had no idea.

Among other things, Family Night was also a way of wearing us down before bedtime through the repeated playing of charades. Each Thursday my dad would come home from working at what he and my mom called "the bomb factory," and he'd type out the agenda on the powder blue Smith-Corona. The schedule usually looked like this:

LISICK FAMILY NIGHT

Pajamas

Questionnaire

Charades

Dessert!

The first item was a given, although it should be noted that my parents participated in this part as well. We were a family of five, entirely clad in pajamas, in a suburban, split-level, tract home at dusk.

Questionnaire was always up for grabs. Any member of the family was free to ask a question of another family member, but there were months at a stretch when my brothers and I would demand to know what my dad did at work all day. "First I get my coffee," he'd start. "And then I read my mail. Sometimes Luke from the office down the hall comes by. . . ." His deflection strategy worked. He'd bore us until we stopped listening and forget by the next week that we had ever asked.

Charades was the rowdiest part of Family Night. Lacking worldly knowledge, we were forced to repeat the same clues, usually drawing from the worlds of Walt Disney, Dr. Seuss, or daytime television. A quick batch of jumping jacks was enough to act out the *Jack LaLanne Show*, the early morning exercise program we watched religiously as we scarfed down our Pop Tarts, and my mom's specialty was a surprisingly nuanced version of Dick Van Dyke's Bert the Chimney Sweep from *Mary Poppins*.

4

We were obsessed with *Mary Poppins*. My oldest brother Paul, at the age of seven, had already typed out a sixty-five page sequel about what Jane and Michael Banks do after Mary leaves—namely, horse racing and international spying. And I was in the annoying, precocious habit of blurting out "supercalifragilisticexpealidocious!" any time something favorable happened, like dismounting the backyard trapeze without doing a face-plant or remembering to pull down my underwear before I peed. We'd clamor for Mom to keep up the Bert routine even as we moved on to the dessert portion of the evening, demanding that she jump up and kick her heels together as she emerged from the kitchen with a plate of quivering, red Jell-O squares arranged like a ramshackle Quonset hut.

It took only one neighborhood block party—at which I spent all afternoon marveling at men with bushy muttonchop sideburns and ladies with crocheted halter tops—to figure out that our family was seriously out of step. To quote Sammy Davis Jr., whose hit single "The Candy Man" was in heavy rotation on our turntable, "We were four corners, man." We were squares.

Then, one Thursday evening, a mystery item appeared on the agenda. There, after "Dessert," was typed "???" A million possibilities flashed through my mind, including a brand new Dough Boy swimming pool, unlimited Ding Dongs, and a surprise visit from Speed Racer. Our tiny brains were fully torquing. We'd just spooned the nondairy, whipped topping on our Jell-O when my dad gave my mom the go ahead. She looked excited, like she had last Christmas when she found the brand new vacuum cleaner with the hose attachments under the tree.

"Next week," she announced, "Nancy Patton is going to move in with us!"

The words were barely out of her mouth before we all started jumping around the living room and hugging each other like we'd recently seen the men's Olympic swim team doing poolside in Munich. Nancy Patton was our favorite babysitter, a teenager with wild clothes and hair so long I often requested she demonstrate how she could sit on it—pulling it back from her shoulders, folding it under her hip-huggers, and pulling it through her crotch. She would be our braless Mary Poppins in platform shoes! Instead of singing "A Spoonful of Sugar" while we cleaned up the nursery, we could air jam to Led Zeppelin and learn to throw frisbees. Years later, we found out that the reason Nancy moved in was because her mother had just committed suicide, her brother was fighting in Vietnam, and her father was some kind of asshole. At the time, we just saw her as our ticket out of Squaresville.

The following week, Nancy had been in the house twenty minutes, and already things were heating up, literally, as she sparked up some frankincense and lined her window sill with tall, purple candles. We brought our Legos into her new bedroom and stayed there all afternoon, watching her string beads from the door frame and toss sheer scarves over lamp shades. I was convinced she was some kind of genius, as exotic as Cher, just not as scary. Plus, she called us dude. "Hey, dude!" she'd say, making me feel as important as her teenage friends, although I was just a couple years out of diapers. "Where did you stash all your crayons, dude?" When my parents finally pried us out of Nancy's bedroom at the end of the day, my brother Chris and I snuck back to her with our blankets after bedtime, falling asleep, keeping vigil.

My brothers and I weren't the only ones transformed by Nancy's presence. My parents may have been old-fashioned, but their Midwestern enthusiasm and acceptance of others went a long way. Just weeks after Nancy moved in, my mom got a new hairstyle for the first time in ten years. Not that the enormous, bulbous Afro-style perm looked good on her, but the fact that she was willing to trade in her hairbrush for a large plastic pick was admirable.

My dad was a bit slower with his experimentation, but once his birthday came around and Nancy presented him with a hand-tooled leather belt, adorned with colorful butterflies, flowers, and fat, yellow bumblebees, he caught the fashion bug. He reserved his earth shoes for the weekend, but the fulsome mustache that hovered over his lip went with him everywhere.

Another bonus of having Nancy around was that I finally gained access to some of the other houses in the neighborhood—most importantly, the ones with teenagers in them. I'd wait all day for her to get home from school, biding my time with napping and Chutes and Ladders, until we could disappear together into someone's shag-carpeted Eichler home. We'd hang out with Pam and

Tam Davis, twins who wore cutoff shorts and were always barefoot, or the Lees, a Chinese Hawaiian family who had a kiddie pool full of sugarcane to munch on in their backyard. *Just stay mellow*, I'd tell myself, surrounded by groovy high schoolers lounging on beanbags, *and they won't realize you're four.*

With a live-in babysitter, my mom and dad started going out on dates a little more, although they always seemed to be home before it got dark out. On those nights, instead of bedtime stories, we'd be on the receiving end of my mom's capsule movie reviews—*American Graffiti*: "It was just like high school! Only they make it a bit wilder 'cause it's the movies and all." *The Sting*: "I can understand why some women go for Robert Redford, but for my money, Paul Newman is the most handsome man in Hollywood!"

One Saturday morning, my dad called a meeting after breakfast. They had gone to The City the night before, meaning all the way into San Francisco. (The City was a mystery, somewhere I hadn't been yet, but I noticed all of my parents' rare trips there were preceded by a week's worth of discussion about parking, maps, safety, money, and the best place to get clam chowder in a hollowed-out loaf of sourdough bread.) We gathered in the living room, Nancy too, and my dad explained that they had something very important to tell us.

"Last night in The City," my mom said, "we saw something very, very special." She then pulled out the program to the Andrew Lloyd Webber musical, *Jesus Christ Superstar*.

"You may have heard of people called the hippies," my dad said, scanning our faces for any sign of recognition. "They usually have long hair, even the men, and they look a little different from regular people."

"And they are great singers and dancers," my mom added. My dad looked vaguely annoyed with this comment, but Nancy backed her up.

"It's true, Ron." I loved how Nancy called him Ron, like they were on the same level. "Music is important to the movement," she said, pulling her hair up into a swatch of leather and fastening it with a chopstick. Dreamy.

My dad continued, "Sometimes people are judged on what they look like instead of who they really are." I wondered if his new facial hair had contributed to his heightened sensitivity. "We just want you kids to know that if you see someone who looks scary or strange . . ."

"Well, not too scary or strange," my mom interrupted. "Not a crazy person talking crazy talk."

"Right," my dad said. "Not one of the crazies, but just someone a little different. Keep in mind that this person could be a nice person at heart."

"Or," my mom added, her eyes wide with possibility, "they could even be Jesus."

This went on to become a running joke in my family. Whenever we witnessed some kind of human spectacle, say a nose-picking homunculus sputtering by on an ailing moped or a grandmother in a mangy wig arguing with a squirrel, I'd look to my parents and say wistfully, "Mom and Dad, is that Jesus?"

They'd pretend to be scandalized, but secretly they were fascinated that sacrilege even occurred to me. The most subversive thing they had ever done was move to California (dwarfing the first runner-up—my mom's one pre-legal Rob Roy at a bar in Chicago) and yet somehow these devout Catholics wound up with a daughter who was making fun of Jesus by the time she was enrolled in kindergarten. Was it all the TV? Too much sun? Nancy? However I got that way, my parents never seemed overly concerned about it, just amused and curious—like wondering how that big schooner got into that tiny bottle.

It was a big blow for everyone a year later when Nancy moved out to go to college, especially because Family Night had really kicked into high gear once she arrived. Instead of shunning our uncool pajama party, she had participated with a wild fervor that I've since learned isn't all that unusual among uninhibited hippies, but it made a lasting impression on me. When I suggested that we immediately get a new hippie to replace Nancy, my parents refused, airing out her room and turning it into an office so my mom could start tutoring children with learning disabilities. Didn't they care about anyone?

The next Thursday after she moved out, my dad took a vote at the dinner table. Who was in favor of continuing Family Night without Nancy? My brothers and I looked at one another, not sure how to proceed. It didn't seem right to keep doing it without her.

"No matter what happens," my mom said, making eye contact with each of us, "I will always make Jell-O for you whenever you ask."

And that sealed it. Family Night was dead. Long live Family Night.

② LADIES' LUNCHEON

The funniest piece of mail I get all year, the one that I can't believe is actually addressed to me, arrives sometime during the first week of December and is decorated with a tasteful yuletide icon. Not a bloated red Santa or stubby little elf, but something more along the lines of a stark solitary reindeer in profile, staring ahead, focused on the business at hand. Simple. Classy. The kind of new minimalism that everyone has figured out is usually in good taste. I don't even need to open the envelope because I know for a fact that it reads: "Kathy's Annual Ladies' Luncheon. Please arrive by noon and bring a gift for the gift exchange. Regrets only."

There's no need to check the date either. Kathy's Annual Ladies' Luncheon is always the Sunday before Christmas, unless of course Christmas falls on a Monday, as it did in the year 2000. And the years 1995, 1989, and 1978. I know because I was there all of those years. From 1976 to, and including, last year, I have attended twenty-eight Ladies' Luncheons hosted by Kathy Sheridon, the mother of my childhood best friend, Amy.

That first year, my family had just moved into our new neighborhood, a place where actual signs enforced the fact that its official name was Prides Crossing. Kathy summoned me and Amy for a meeting in her specially appointed Crafts Room, an extension off the garage where she would go for hours at a time to work on her latest projects. As the paint dried on a platoon of clothespin toy soldiers behind her, she informed us that the following Sunday we should plan on working all day at her party. "Let me check with my mom," I said, while she poked a hole in each end of an egg with a needle and blew the contents into a glass bowl. She blotted her lips with a handkerchief and started on another egg. "I've already cleared it with her. You're good to go." Amy looked over at me and shrugged. Kathy ruled the roost at her house, so why shouldn't she also be in charge over at mine.

Kathy finished up her egg project and led us back into the house for a run-through. First, we'd be at the ready when the doorbell rang to present each woman with a hand-calligraphed name tag. We were then to offer her a glass of champagne punch. The punch bowl should always be filled at least halfway—one part ginger ale to two parts champagne—and there were more ice ring molds in the freezer. Important was the fact that Mrs. Clark would not be having the punch, and we should refrain from offering her any. She, for some reason, would be having Martinelli's Sparkling Cider only.

We were then to direct the ladies to put their gifts for the gift exchange under the tree. We would wait until we received the signal to seat all the ladies for lunch. Mr. Sheridon, in his only appearance that day, would be responsible for decanting the wine from a large box into empty bottles with a different wine label on them. Then we were to plate and deliver the salads. These were followed by slices of quiche, which were to be presented with the tip of the triangle toward the lady, making it much more inviting to eat.

After we cleared the plates, it would be time to bring tea or coffee and take dessert orders. The choices were Barbara O'Malley's pecan pie, Elaine Taylor's chocolate mousse cake, Kathy Seal's lemon meringue pie, Sharon Walsh's shortbread cookies, and my mom's almond pound cake. We should be aware that a guest might want to sample more than one dessert, so we should try to slice the pies and cakes in sixteenths or at least twelfths. Next we would clear dessert plates while the ladies got ready for the gift exchange. Finally, we would wash all the Christmas Spode lunch plates. If we finished in time, we could come into the sunken living room and watch the gift exchange, after which we would clean up all the wrapping paper. For this we were to be paid five dollars. We were eight years old.

The day of that first party, Amy and I were understandably excited. We were about to spend all day with thirty suburban moms! We took our job extremely seriously and flitted around the house like Dickensian waifs, our brows furrowed, eager to please. Of course, it being 1976, instead of working away in soot-covered rags,

I was sporting some kind of fun red, white, and blue sweater vest. Amy, also clad in the patriotic colors so popular that year, was wearing a jumpsuit that was "handmade from scratch." At a time when crafts were having such a renaissance in the culture, it was becoming increasingly important to find out who had made what with their own two hands, and how long it had taken them. Kathy, of course, was the queen bee of this sort of thing, excelling at both craft-making and quizzing others about their commitment to craft.

A couple hours into the party I was really on a roll. I served from the left, cleared from the right, and for the one and only time in my life, memorized orders for a table of twelve. I'm sure my mom was wondering what had gotten into me, but she had to have seen it in my eyes: my fear of Kathy. I didn't know a mom could be like that—so alpha. Kathy was Martha Stewart when Martha Stewart was busy getting into stocks—the first time around. Kathy not only sewed clothes, but also made quilts from the fabric scraps, and then made patchwork teddy bears from the scraps of the scraps. She carved wooden elephants, cultivated an herb garden, and helped Mr. Sheridon build the new redwood hot tub as seen in the pages of *Sunset* magazine. On top of it all, she held down a full-time job working the night shift as an ER nurse at El Camino Hospital.

When we had finished clearing the tables, Kathy gave us a raised eyebrow, and we scurried to usher the ladies into the living room for the gift exchange. Amy circulated with a basket of numbers to determine the order in which the gifts would be opened while I picked up a dish towel and started furiously drying wine glasses. The ten-foot-tall fir tree was overflowing with beautifully wrapped presents, which we had been scoping out all afternoon. I peered in from the kitchen.

"Hey, Bef!" Amy called to me from underneath the dining room table. Amy's habit of sucking on her big toe had produced an astonishing set of buck teeth. Therefore, I was Bef, wif whom she played games like Troof or Dare. I didn't laugh at her teef. The first week I moved in, Mark Dwyer, a sixth grader, had led the neighborhood boys in a chant of "Buck Tooth Beaver! Buck Tooth Beaver!" until I kicked him where it counts and got the nickname The Nutcracker.

I crawled underneath the table, and we finished up our side work, tying gold ribbons around each of the party favors, little hand-painted angel ornaments. I thought I had at last become invisible until I saw Kathy's hand reach down and pick up an ornament off the rug.

"More like this," I heard her voice say as she lifted up the tablecloth and handed me the angel, retied with perfect, even loops. Then I finally had a moment to relax, let down my Dorothy Hamill bowl cut a little, and watch the drama play out.

The details and intricacies of the gift exchange are now legend in certain circles of our town. The rules were—and still are—that everyone places her present anonymously under the tree and then draws a number. Guest #1 can open any present she chooses, and Guest #2 can either steal that present or open a new one. Guest #3 can steal Guest #1 or Guest #2's gift and so on. The third time a present is stolen, it becomes frozen, and the person with the last number can either exchange her gift for one of the unfrozen ones or choose to keep hers. It quickly becomes very complicated and takes up the larger part of the afternoon. Kathy ruled over the proceedings with an iron oven mitt.

Like the single sad Christmas tree left in the lot or the deformed pumpkin on Halloween, the Charlie Brown-ish moment inevitably comes when your present isn't picked until dead last. Exactly twenty-nine gifts have been selected by a jury of your peers, and your gift, either because it's small, or the box got smashed in the trunk, or your wrapping paper is cheap and unattractive, is left there to mock you. The stakes get higher as the game goes on, and none of the seasoned vets wants her present to be the proverbial poop in the champagne flute.

What everyone is going for is a big deal "star of the party" present that gets opened to unrestrained gasps and general mom mayhem. There's usually only one a year. It's a gift that makes everyone go aflutter, immediately demanding to know who brought it and if she made it herself, at home, from scratch, with her own two hands, after laboring over it since Memorial Day weekend. If the proud gift giver did not make it herself, she can still savor the moment by sitting up a little taller in her wingback chair and explaining the story about how she and her husband were traveling through the Amish country on their way to her niece's wedding in Scranton and honestly, we almost missed the sign for the place, but then we saw them. This man and his wife drove one of those buggies like you see in the movies, had *the most perfect skin*, and were selling these gorgeous dolls. So plain really. But so beautiful and *stark*. Well, we fell in love with this little farmer doll. How could you not? The Amish people do everything as if it were the beginning of time.

At this point, someone would be bold enough to ask if she could remove the pants to see if the little farmer was signed—and, if he was, there was a whole new round of excitement. Two more unwritten rules were that Kathy brought the best gift, if only because the man hours she racked up in her Crafts Room were superhuman, and it was always understood that she'd bring the best gift away from the party because *you never steal from Kathy*.

Now it's 1991, seventeen Ladies' Luncheons later. I am staying at my parents' house while I look for an apartment in San Francisco. This is my first year being invited to the party as a Lady. From the beginning, Amy and I had been promised that one day, after we graduated from college, we would be Kathy's guests. It really kept me going all those times I was close to dropping out. I'd sit in my dorm room and think, "If I don't write this paper on Andrea Dworkin's *Pornography: The New Terrorism*, I will never experience the joy of stealing a holly-themed, hand-thrown tea set from Mrs. Whelan in the fourteenth round. Keep writing!!"

Amy, apparently, didn't see the party as much of a dangling carrot. While I had earned my diploma the previous spring, Amy was hung up on some stupid math credit, and, according to her mom, was technically not a college graduate. Thus she was relegated to work the luncheon. When I rang the bell, I was greeted by my lifelong best friend handing me my own calligraphed name tag that had a pink angel holding a bugle on it, captured mid-herald. Flanking Amy were two girls from the neighborhood, our erstwhile replacements, who were about eight or nine years old. Their mothers were attending the lunch for the first time. Kathy was always good about bringing in some new blood each year, to keep things interesting, but this time it really smacked of shady dealings. She invited these ladies to get to their kids.

I had more important things on my mind than Amy's little minions, however. The night before, I had gone to a party in San Francisco where I didn't know too many people and ended up standing around the keg with some older dude. He was just back from Russia, where he'd been working on a project that dealt with the dismantling of Chernobyl, and was about to head off to China to try to overhaul their outdated energy system. Maybe he was intrigued by my chitchat about the finer points of working in the service industry, but you can't really look back once the sun has come up and you're naked at his place doing shots of slivovitz, 138 proof plum-flavored firewater from Bohemia. Clearly, I blacked out because the next thing I remember it was eleven o'clock in the morning, and he was all showered and bringing me coffee and pastries on a tray in bed. I believe he had already gone for a run. I'd never slept with a man who exercised before.

I knew I wasn't supposed to be there. And somehow an errant synapse in my fried brainpan alerted me to the fact that if I shouldn't be there, there was somewhere else I should be. I bolted out the door in my crusty underpants. Like I had done every pre-Christmas Sunday for the previous sixteen years, I would be going to the ladies' luncheon.

I hit the 101 back down toward San Jose, alcohol oozing from my pores, my breath smelling like a family of gnomes had crawled in my mouth and died. Around Mountain View it dawned on me that I hadn't even bought a present for the gift exchange. I was so cocky that all my years of observation would allow me to choose the perfect gift that I decided to slack on it until that morning, convinced I could walk into any "tasteful" boutique and pluck a winner from the shelves. I pulled off the freeway in a freak-out and sped into some minimall where I tried to assess which would be more appropriate: the dry cleaners or the travel agency. Shit! Maybe a gift certificate to the tanning salon? Was that Linda Evans Fitness Center open yet?

I saw a florist across the street and made a run for it. A display of enormous wreaths caught my eye. They were alpine fir, the usual, but then—oh my God—I saw one made from dried chili peppers. The whole Southwest thing was really swinging into force with suburban decorators that year. This could be perfect! I wrenched the display from the wall and put my credit card on the counter, watching my hands tremble on the way down. I was so dehydrated that I was breathing heavily through my mouth like a dog, as if I could sap some moisture from the cool December air. Sixty-three dollars poorer, I got back in my truck and on the freeway, peeled off at my exit, and swung by a drugstore to buy wrapping paper. Incredibly, I pulled up to Kathy's house only fifteen minutes late, but then blew it by spending another ten in the bed of my pickup, wrestling with the wreath until it succumbed to an entire roll of scotch tape. It looked pretty crappy, but much worse was the fact that I could sense some of the ladies staring out at me through the picture window.

Now, in the Hollywood version of this story, I would step into a showcase home filled with all these rich society ladies with face-lifts—and I'd be some kind of urban primitive in a wild getup or a punk rocker with classically "crazy" hair—and everything would stop. But the truth is the other guests were just nice upper-middle-class ladies, mostly nurses and teachers married to scientists or engineers. They get dressed up for the luncheon, but they are the type of ladies who wear the red, mixed-fiber sweater set adorned with a big Christmas tree and shoes that are sensible in all respects except for the embedded multicolored rhinestones. A few of the wilder ladies wear earrings that are flashing tree ornaments. My look was just sloppy, disheveled, and terrible. My hair was a bad home-peroxide job that had turned crispy and yellow. And this was back in the days when I never looked in the mirror except from the front, so I'd walk around with no idea that the back of my hair was all matted and lumpy.

I arrived at the door, thinking that at least I looked better than I felt, but I was really smelly and sore. Amy was too busy managing her team of second graders to notice, so I quickly found my mom and apologized about not calling, telling her that I might have had one glass of wine too many and decided not to drive. Of course, my mom being my mom skipped the lecture about how she had worried or how I'd screwed up her plans and excessively congratulated me on my good judgment. She handed me a champagne punch and, although my stomach was churning, I took it and gulped it down. And then I started reeling. I tried to slip away to the bathroom, but my mom was smoothing down my hair and dabbing at my smeared lipstick, saying that if I had at least stopped by home first she would have been happy to have ironed my pants for me.

The room was a swirl of festive ladies and, for the life of me, I couldn't remember whose daughter got divorced, whose son had a baby, and which of them had a breast cancer scare or had a husband go through chemo. I was blowing it. Dazed, I was just nodding along like I should be back in the kitchen defrosting another ice ring. I milled around some more, attempting to "look normal" as I eased myself into conversations about vacation homes in Tahoe, the Oakland fires, rose pruning, the De Anza flea market, gallbladder surgery, and how great Nick Nolte was in *The Prince of Tides*. Barbra, as usual, was also fantastic.

People were trying to chitchat about What I Want To Do With My Life, but I was twenty-one years old, I had just gotten out of college, and the conversation made me feel like I should've been submerged in a pool with scuba gear on—like Dustin Hoffman in *The Graduate*. Finally, a roiling debate ensued about whether stuffing is better inside or outside of the turkey, and I got a window to go to the bathroom. I plunged my red, blotchy face into a sink full of water, and when I looked in the mirror, at least twenty minutes after I had been chatting, nodding empathetically, and laughing whenever I thought it was appropriate, I saw something stuck between my two front teeth. Closer inspection revealed it to be a curly, black pubic hair—right there between my central and lateral incisors. This was a first for me.

Amy came and rounded us up to take our seats for lunch. I couldn't help but notice that the second graders were totally useless, following her around like puppies. Where was the initiative in these kids? Where was the sense of commitment? One kid actually had a Gameboy, and I could already tell by the look on Kathy's face that she had axed them off the list for the next year.

The lunch was something of a haze, if only because of the chardonnay that had become the only drink option when Kathy realized some years ago that no one ever wanted anything else (except Mrs. Clark who drank tap water). The only other thing I remember—besides Mrs. Curran's pride over the fact that her boys were not living with their girlfriends before marriage or that one of the second graders set down my quiche incorrectly—was that one woman, new that year, apropos of nothing, leaned forward and said, "Let me tell you ladies something! I love having an affair with a married man because it's always special-event time!" I had just spent all night screwing a stranger, and even I was scandalized. For the first time ever, I felt a little camaraderie with the rest of the ladies, who proceeded to clear their throats and readjust their napkins until someone mentioned how much better traffic is going to be now that the new freeway is built, and everyone agreed.

When Amy announced it was now time for the gift exchange, I sat on the floor and settled in for three more hours of fun, as Kathy, my mom, and the other twenty-five guests took their distinguished places in the chairs circling the living room. All of us picked our numbers, and I eyed my present hiding in the back against the fireplace. Interesting, I thought, that although I had arrived last and set mine down toward the front of the pile, it had mysteriously been moved to a less conspicuous location.

The first few rounds went pretty smoothly. My mom had one of the early numbers and scored a huge ceramic Italian bowl, one of the few presents I would actually want for myself and which we soon found out was purchased in a small town in Tuscany from a very large woman who lost her husband in the Franco-Italian War. Of course, my mother had to relinquish the bowl to Mrs. Collins, who presented a little speech about her semester abroad in Rome before snatching the prized item away. My turn came, and I opened an incredibly haunting Santa cookie jar, which was manufactured by a respectable company, but clearly freaked people out with its ghostly white body, demonic expression, and eerie red splotches on its nose and cheeks that looked like splattered blood. At one point, Amy, who stood hand-drying glass after glass in the doorway after her "helpers" had plopped down in the living room with the ladies, mouthed me the question, "Is that one yours?" I looked over at the remaining pile, seeing that as the gifts dwindled, my mental-institution-wrapping job was becoming more and more exposed.

Then I started to get really nervous. I had sat through year after year of cringe-worthy, gift-opening moments. I prided myself on knowing what goes over and what gets whispered about later. Whenever a repeat guest (first-timers always brought the wrong gift) showed up with a plastic Santa and Mrs. Claus salt and pepper set or a box of tacky ornaments, I always wondered what kind of psychological-attention disorder she had. What could have compelled her to bring something so overtly cheap and inappropriate? What kind of gall does it take to show up with a set of red and green candles, as one guest infamously did, and walk away with a six-foot-long, hand-quilted banner, inscribed with the word "Noel," made by the gift giver's aunt who spent all summer slaving over it from the confines of her convent? You've got to pay to play at Kathy's Ladies' Luncheon.

The end times were obviously coming for me. No one had ever brought a wreath before, and now I realized it was dumb to introduce an untested specimen into a world where only angels, reindeer, Santas, snowmen, and the occasional nutcracker played. Only four gifts were left, and mine sat there looking like a toddler had snuck down on Christmas morning, unwrapped it with his teeth, and tried to put it back together before his parents woke up.

Just when I was about to pass a note to my mom, demanding that if she had another of her gifts stolen, she was morally obligated to go and open mine, something extraordinary happened. A cheery

26

human resources manager (who was new that year and had brought an embarrassing basket of potpourri) grabbed my gift exclaiming, to my delight, "I like mine big and messy!" I could feel the tension in the room. "Who brought this one?" Kathy asked suspiciously, which, to my knowledge has never happened in the history of her parties. It must have looked really bad because you at least wait until you see what's inside before you pin the perp. I closed my eyes and raised my hand. And then all I heard was the sound of Amy laughing in the kitchen with her dad.

When the red chili pepper wreath was unveiled, a hush went across the room and everyone turned to Kathy to gauge her reaction. Kathy, of course, the arbiter of home decorating with crafts, was too busy staring at the wreath in disbelief to notice the attention. "It's wonderful!" she blurted, and her pure reaction garnered a round of applause for me. When the hubbub subsided, she just had to ask, "Did you get it in Santa Fe?"

I was tempted to say yes and embark on a tale involving a cattle ranch, a monk, and a blind Pueblo spirit guide, but I refrained. I needed to sit tight with my victory. But then, when Kathy's turn came, she pulled the final coup. She got up from her chair, strutted across the floor, and grabbed the wreath—instantly absolving me of my awful hygiene, inappropriate wardrobe, subpar social skills, and slurred speech. I walked out a hero. Now if only somebody on eBay would buy that creepy albino cookie jar.

③
DIDN'T I ALMOST HAVE IT ALL?

The summer before high school, I decided to spend my vacation with a singular focus and pursuit. It was time to put an end to the constant dicking around, the elaborate prank phone call sessions, the aborted sewing projects, the hustling for a buck by ironing my dad's handkerchiefs, all while trying to get my doorbell-cleaning business off the ground in between bouts of heavy TV watching. I had friends who were traveling to Europe, volunteering to change bedsheets at the retirement home, and tackling a reading list provided by their freshman English teachers, but that wasn't my style. I mean the effort part. I got A's and B's without studying, was decent at sports without practicing, and landed a minor role in the junior high musical, *Little Mary Sunshine*, with my mediocre voice. Even my hair feathered without a lot of hassle. I was consistently described as "well-rounded," but I was starting to believe that there was nothing as well-rounded as an absolute zero. At fourteen, it looked like I was on the fast track to a career in real estate or public relations. I figured all it would take to divert such a disaster was a little more focus.

From movies and television, I'd learned that the smartest way for teens to succeed was by making personal sacrifices and then steeling themselves against the jealous naysayers who would inevitably want to bring them down, especially if it meant losing friends and learning a lesson along the way. In the short amount of time it took for a montage scene to depict someone repeatedly breaking wood blocks with bare feet or teaching the blind girl to run hurdles, an important change would occur. When the mid-tempo pop score moved into its slow fade, they could almost smell the victory. The heroes now had all the components to make them whole and could begin dealing with new concerns, like polishing trophies, receiving fan mail, or convincing their friends over a hot lunch in the cafeteria that they hadn't changed. "Maybe it's you that's changed," I practiced saying into the reflection of our swimming pool as I floated aimlessly on a chewed-up raft. Then it came to me. After kicking around a few ideas, including jam making and poetry, I was savvy enough to pick something at which I'd already shown some aptitude. I would concentrate on extreme tanning.

I had a pretty impressive base color going and figured, with a little effort, I could really make a go of it. The schedule would be grueling; I knew that. No more drawing the shades in the family room to settle in for a Channel 44 marathon of *Petticoat Junction* into *Andy Griffith* into *Mr. Ed* into *Gomer Pyle* into *Gilligan's Island* into *I Dream of Jeannie* into *Leave it to Beaver*, with an occasional chaser of *All My Children* thrown in. This was serious business. I bought my own can of Crisco and a personal roll of aluminum foil and began developing an involved rotation system that required not only slight adjustments on the quarter hour, but also a protracted journey from the south side of the swimming pool to the north side—a distance of about fifty feet that took me nearly eight hours to cover. Stoically dragging the lounge chair behind me across the pebbled patio, my resemblance to Christ was obvious, if only He'd had a hand free for a tube of lip gloss and a mayonnaise jar full of iced Tab. Perhaps I took a few breaks throughout the day. I seem to remember sandwiches and some important phone calls, but mostly I concentrated on the task at hand. For the first time in my life, I was really working hard, and it was satisfying.

My favorite part of the job was not how my skin took on the burnished burl hue of the truly precancerous, but the path of discovery. It amazed me to realize that my mind could be so blank day after day for the better parts of June, July, and August. There was nothing going on up there at all. If I had been smarter or more self-conscious, I might have known to attribute at least part of my slacking to the study of Zen, like so many people I would meet later in life. But that thought, along with a fathomless host of others, didn't even pass through my brain. Being "present" and "in the moment" was just part and parcel of what we called "laying out," as in:

MOM: What are you going to do today, honey?

ME: I'm just going to lay out.

MOM: Okay.

Eight hours later . . .

DAD: How was your day?

ME: Good. I laid out.

DAD: You sure got a helluva tan going.

ME: Thanks.

I wasn't sure how it would fly at first, but laying out appeared to be a perfectly acceptable hobby in my family, akin to Paul's private Latin instruction and Chris's debate tournaments. I may have quit piano, soccer, and gymnastics, but no one could argue that I had trouble applying myself once I set my mind to a goal. I was tan, and then I got tanner—success.

When the new school year rolled around, my mind-blowing tan became my calling card. In the months since we graduated from eighth grade, braces came off, short boys grew taller, and training bras developed into C cups, but no one had made such leaps and bounds in the tanning department. I felt great, if not a little anxious about what was going to happen now that the days were growing shorter, and all my daylight hours were being wasted in a classroom under fluorescent lights.

A few weeks into the school year, I realized just how much

power a tan could wield when it was announced that I was one of five nominees for freshman homecoming princess. I was neither excited nor horrified, just a little confused. Aside from my reckless foray into the world of melanin adjustment, I didn't feel that much different. And yet, clearly, I was now somebody my classmates could actually picture riding around the football field at halftime in the back of a brand new convertible Cabriolet owned by Kelly Sampson's mom, a tennis nut with a radical boob job. Here's a look at the competition:

Krista Gregory: What a little lady! Krista was always impeccably dressed in the latest teen fashions, and she was incredibly nice to everyone. The fact that some people thought she was phony would be nullified by the sympathy card based on rumors that her mother started bleaching Krista's hair blond as soon as it started to go dark—when she was eight years old.

Tanya Olson: Straight-A student involved in community projects and her church. I think the people who voted for her are now history professors, avant-garde musicians, software developers, and heads of nonprofit arts centers and educational foundations, etc. She was smart and cool, but I remember sincerely thinking, "She wears glasses. There's no way she'll win."

Julie Hartman: A living doll with brains to match. I love an adorable airhead as much as anyone, and how much street smarts are you supposed to have when your street is a cul-de-sac called

Country Club Court? But I truly believed she was just too dumb to be a princess.

Cecilia Bari: Even tanner than me, but it is important to point out that her tan was aided by the fact that she is half-Sicilian. She was mostly popular because of her really long hair—the kind of long that only a teenager can get away with. When you see an adult with hair this long, down to their knees and frayed into an inverted triangle at the ends, you have to start counting in mental problems. Anyway, it was still 1984 at this point. Multicultural exoticism wouldn't be embraced by white suburban teens for many years to come. No chance.

On the day the final votes were cast, I had a doctor's appointment to get an infected mole removed from my back and missed the voting. My mom took me out to McDonald's afterward, and as I sat eating my Happy Meal with a piece of bloody gauze nestled between my shoulder blades, I entertained the thought of actually winning the crown. What would it mean? There were no real duties associated with being a member of the royal court, at least as far as I could tell. The homecoming princess just rode around the football field at halftime, went to a dance in the gym later, and received a free bouquet of roses.

When I returned to school in the afternoon, the votes were being tallied in the office. I have no recollection of an official announcement being made—this shows how ambivalent I was—but it turned out that I won. The following week, I would be standing on the football field, my arm interlocked with David Friedman, the homecoming prince. Immediately, the dread set in. *I just know I am going to be one of those people who peak in high school,* I thought, waiting for the carpool mom to pick me up out front. *I am reaching the apex of my powers shortly before learning to drive, and then I'll bottom out in college when different brands of identity like intelligence, humor, creativity, and contrived eccentricity start to mean more than a hot tan or a nice rack.* I was doomed.

What made matters even worse was that suddenly all sorts of new people came sniffing around: the football players and cheerleaders with their convertible cars and the party girls and surfer boys with their puka shells. I already had Amy and Nicole, my two friends since elementary school. I didn't want any more friends. I was curious about the popular people, but slightly terrified. I'd seen their marijuana leaf T-shirts and knew they hung out in the smoking section next to the auto shop. I'd heard the rumors about something called Bartles & Jaymes. Yet, I wasn't against using my new social standing for personal gain because I definitely had my sights set high. I wanted to go on a date with Kyle Anderson.

Kyle Anderson was a senior and the older brother of one of my brother's friends. He was raised in a career military family and had a formality about him that I found odd and appealing. He would greet me in the hallway between classes by shaking my hand and offering me a stick of Big Red. Tall and handsome, he was part of the popular jock crowd and yet different from them in a way that I romanticized. He was one of the insiders but still on the outside. Kind of like what Sammy Davis Jr. was to the Rat Pack, except Kyle wasn't black, Jewish, or short. But I noticed he did have a certain sway with the ladies.

After extensively observing him one night in a pizza parlor from a corner booth with Amy and Nicole, I saw how the popular senior girls fawned all over him, but then ran back to their boyfriends giggling. Obviously, his maturity and intelligence were far too intimidating for those girls. Those pretty party girls were not interesting or worldly enough for him, I decided, picking cheese out of my retainer and checking my watch to make sure I didn't miss my 10:00 P.M. curfew.

How I actually snared the coveted date with Kyle I'll never know, but I have a feeling it was the result of some sort of humiliating note passing or hint dropping that I've since blocked out. All I know is that the Monday before homecoming, we had the following exchange in the breezeway:

KYLE: [shaking my hand] Miss Lisick!
ME: Mr. Anderson.
KYLE: How would you like to go out to dinner this Saturday night?
ME: Hey, that'd be great!
KYLE: I'm escorting Leslie Egan to the homecoming game the night before, and I don't have to return the tuxedo until Monday. How about I wear that, you wear your homecoming dress, and I'll take you someplace nice.

36

ME: Great!

KYLE: [*He reaches into his pocket.*] Big Red?

I walked away excited and also extremely impressed that he was escorting Leslie Egan, the head cheerleader whose boyfriend was unable to escort her due to his quarterback duties that evening. Leslie had the most incredible hair. She'd blow-dry her huge mane of hair all over to the left side and constantly hold her head at a forty-five degree angle to keep it there. The effect was as if a giant wind machine was constantly tracking her from just off her right shoulder, a wind machine so powerful that it not only blew her hair in a giant, asymmetrical cascade, but also upset the natural alignment of her neck with the rest of her spinal column, like she was a cyborg honing in on a high-pitched frequency in the distance.

It was two days before homecoming, and I hadn't even started looking for a dress. What was wrong with me? I became paralyzed by the thought of having everyone looking at me. They would see me up there on display and instantly decide that they liked me better before, back when they voted for me. Now that I was actually the homecoming princess, it would be obvious that I had spent the last week becoming stuck-up and conceited. Most of the dresses I owned were from thrift stores, 1950s chiffon prom dresses or loud 1960s shifts. I couldn't wear those because then it would look like I thought I was all cool and different, trying to stand out even more. I also knew I didn't want to wear anything sexy because I was only a freshman. The older girls would surely slut it up for everyone. They always did. My mom had been pleading with me all week to let her take me to the mall, and I had kept putting her off. Now I was screwed.

The afternoon before the big day I came home from school and saw a dress hanging in plastic in the front hallway. Not only was it plaid, but the colors included (but were not limited to) royal blue, lime green, canary yellow, bright pink, and various shades of purple. The sleeves were as puffy as two enormous (plaid) clouds of cotton candy.

"What do you think?" my mom asked, handing me a Reese's Peanut Butter Cup. "I got it from Rita in my bridge group."

"Huh," I replied, pulling it off the coat rack, holding it at arm's length and turning it around.

"Her daughter only wore it once. To her prom."

If I remembered correctly, her daughter was old enough to have kids of her own by now, making the dress that perfect awkward age of something that was too new to be retro and too old to be remotely fashionable. She took off the plastic for me, so I could behold its unique color scheme.

"And this," she said, pulling a long sash from the neck of the hanger, "goes around your waist and ties in a big bow in back!"

"Wow," I said, putting a whole peanut butter cup into my mouth, upside down, and holding it there while the crinkled edges melted on my tongue. This was shaping up to be every teenage girl's nightmare.

"Great," I said, as I snorfled. "I'll wear it." And then I went to watch TV.

She followed me through the kitchen. "Well, don't you want to try it on, honey? What about shoes?"

"I'll try it on after *The Brady Bunch* is over."

Later that night, when everyone was asleep, I finally brought the dress back to my room. It was a couple sizes too big and the skirt fell at an awkward length, about mid-calf. I got in my pajamas—a large pair of men's boxers that I would sometimes wear to school as shorts, safety pinning the fly—and went to bed. If people are going to vote for a person like me for homecoming princess, I fell asleep thinking, this is what they're going to get—me wearing whatever dress happened to swoop into my life at just the moment I needed it, no matter how hideous it was.

This is still my MO a lot of the time. When paralyzed by making decisions where all the options are unappealing, I'm able to wait it out for an uncomfortably long time, until the inevitable answer makes itself known to me. It's like constantly having a Mexican standoff with myself. For instance, I recently went to a baby shower for my sister-in-law, and I didn't have a card to go on my gift. Sometimes I will make a card myself if I have something good laying around, like an envelope from an early 1980s Butterick sewing pattern or a sparkly, Hulk Hogan tablecloth, but I refuse to participate in greeting card culture (with occasional exceptions for half-price cards in Spanish or something from the Hallmark Mahogany line for African Americans.) Anyway, my mom had an extra one on her, a standard Hallmark number with an excessive poem that rhymed about little baby hugs and little baby hands, and she said, "Well, you can use this one, but it's not really a 'Beth' card." I cringed, but I took her up on it. It was most definitely a "Beth" card as it was the card that presented itself at the last possible minute. Ugly, yet unde-niably functional—a theme in my life, for sure.

The next afternoon I came home from field hockey practice and watched cartoons like I did every other day. About a half hour before we had to leave for the game, my mom poked her head in and suggested I'd better start getting ready. I looked at the mud caking my inner thighs and was totally bummed out that I would have to take a second shower that day. Maybe I could just sponge down with a washcloth? I contemplated putting on mascara, but decided against it. I never wore it to school, so why would I put it on for this? It seemed fake. Then, without thinking anything of it, not under-standing how wrong this was, I went into my mom's drawer and bor-rowed a pair of black nylon knee-highs from her. I remember her saying how relieved she was when her skirt was long enough not to have to wear pantyhose, and it made sense to me. And then, the capper: I went into her closet and fished out a pair of her sensible, low-heeled, Easy Spirit pumps, which were a full size too big for me. I grabbed some string cheese from the fridge, put on my Walkman, and got in the back of the wood-paneled station wagon.

My parents dropped me off at the front gate, and I stood in line to pay my dollar entrance fee. Everybody was wearing jeans and sweatshirts, and I instantly felt stupid in my oversized, plaid dress and stretched-out mom shoes. I needed to make a mental note to pay more attention to what I wore. I looked around for Kyle, eager to see how dapper he would look in his tux, getting a preview for our big date the next night. That was the real excitement, if I could just get over this hump tonight. I stood around for the entire first half of the football game sharing a tray of nachos with Amy and Nicole, wearing a big sheepskin-lined denim jacket over my dress.

"Maybe we should run behind your convertible and drag you out of it," Nicole said. "We could start whaling on you, beating you up in front of everyone!"

"I'll get some ketchup from the snack shack!" Amy said and ran off.

We had been staging fake catfights, inspired by the TV show *Dynasty*, in public places for a few years. We would stand at busy intersections or out in the quad during lunch break and pretend to pull one another's hair and kick one another in the shins. Inevitably, we would wind up rolling around on the ground until someone stepped in to break it up. But even though I knew this could make it the most memorable homecoming ever, I chickened out. I didn't want to draw any more attention to myself than I had to.

The vice principal, an excitable lady who was also in charge of all factions of the Spirit Squad (which included cheerleaders, drill team, color guard, letter girls, song girls, and mascots) got on her megaphone and called everyone over: "Princes and princesses, kings and queens!"

Just as I was making my way over, some elementary school boys who were running around accidentally dumped an entire Coke on me. It dripped down the front of my dress and puddled at my feet.

"Oh, no!" the sophomore princess cried, embracing me while turning her head in the opposite direction so her makeup didn't smear. "I would kill those little fuckers!"

I laughed and climbed up onto the car. One good thing about that dress was that it certainly didn't show stains.

I finally got a glimpse of Kyle, already in his Mercedes Coupe with his arm around Leslie Egan. She being the Senior Queen, they were in the last car of the procession. Dave and I were in the first car. We were instructed to wave to everyone in the bleachers as we passed, but as the car started to make its way slowly around the track, I was so conflicted. I knew waving looked lame, like we thought we were really special or something, but if I didn't do it, everyone would think I was stuck-up. I thought for a second about doing a fake royal wave, a Miss America thing, but what if people didn't know I was making fun of the wave? I decided it would be better to salute the crowd, a stiff hand angled at my brow, pushing my bangs into my eyes. Perhaps an unconscious nod to my date with Kyle the next night.

Risers had been brought out to the field by members of the marching band, in which my brother Chris served as the only male who played the flute. The following year, tired of being called a fag, he would switch to the more manly double-reeded bassoon. As our names were called, we stepped out of our cars and paraded onto the makeshift stage. People in the stands were cheering wildly as if to say, "We adore you, tan and popular people with decent GPAs!" More waving. Flashbulbs popping. I couldn't wait for it to be over, so it could be tomorrow already. At one point I looked over at Kyle and caught him looking back at me. I imagined him mouthing the words, "Tomorrow will be our night, magic lady! Tomorrow we will soar with the eagles!"

I was up early the next day, already preparing for my date, utilizing a set of guidelines laid out by *Seventeen* magazine. I kept trying to avoid my parents and brothers, sneaking into the pantry for oatmeal, so I could make a facial mask and scoop mayonnaise out of the jar for a special hair conditioner before I settled into a bathtub filled with rose petals. I shaved my legs twice. I kept catching my mom talking on the phone about how this weekend was like my coming out party, with the homecoming and the big first date and all. It was killing me. Why was she making such a big deal out of it, I thought as I reviewed the seven-step process for my eye shadow and narrowed down which pressure points would receive a dab of Loves Baby Soft Fresh Rain Scent. Wrinkled with dried-up Coke, the awkward plaid dress was replaced with a plain, cream-colored, taffeta one that I'd worn once to a dance in junior high. I thought of it as a blank canvas that would come alive once I applied my superior grooming routine and sparkling personality.

Kyle arrived at my house in his rented tuxedo, as advertised, with a single pink rose for me and another one for my mom. If there had been any doubts about sending her fourteen-year-old daughter out on a date with an eighteen-year-old high school senior (and there really hadn't been), that rose for my mom spoke volumes. Kyle was clearly a gentleman whose military use of "Yes, sir" and "No, sir" only supported his case. My mom disappeared into the kitchen to find vases as my brothers, my dad, and I stood around the entry hall. "Now don't keep her out all night!" my dad joked. The look of surprise on Kyle's face sealed the deal. I had found a real winner. Then we went through a roll of film, utilizing all rooms of the house and every possible combination of people.

"Let's get one of Beth, Kyle, and Chris!"

"Okay, now both the older brothers and the date!"

"How about Mom and daughter with Kyle standing behind them?"

"Okay, now I'll get the timer going, and we'll get everybody together by the bougainvillea!"

At last, we walked out into the warm October evening, and Kyle opened the passenger side door of his yellow Datsun B210 for me. I slid in, admiring the way he had replaced the handle of the stick shift with the grip from a ski pole. Very cool. "You look beautiful," he said, handing me a stick of Big Red. "Why didn't you wear that last night instead of that other thing?"

He had made us reservations at the Chart House, a steak house chain whose cachet at this particular location was that it was situated inside an old Victorian house—authentically complete with a hitching post for your horse on the front lawn! We climbed the front steps, and he ushered me in with his hand firmly on the back of my elbow. If I hadn't felt like a princess the night before, stepping into the fanciest steak house chain in the greater Bay Area on the arm of a future military cadet was starting to do it for me.

As the hostess admired our outfits and led us to our table, it occurred to me that I'd never been to a restaurant without somebody's parents before. When the waiter asked what I wanted to drink, my autopilot said, "I'll have a glass of milk, please." Wait, that didn't sound right. Immediately sensing the tension, I changed my order to something more cosmopolitan—a Shirley Temple, which I had heard about in movies.

When our meals arrived, the baked potato sommelier ceremoniously smothered our potatoes with butter, sour cream, chives, cheddar cheese, bacon bits, and freshly ground pepper. I still had to decide if I wanted French, Italian, thousand island, bleu cheese, honey mustard, or poppy seed dressing on my salad. I was in heaven.

"So are you definitely going to West Point next year?" I asked, attempting to cut a piece off of my one-and-a-half pound, three-inch thick porterhouse. I approached the steak gingerly at first, as if I was performing an autopsy, but soon enough I was sawing away like a serial killer dismembering a body.

"Looks like it," he said. "I just need to get the letter of recommendation from the congressman."

I nodded enthusiastically, making eye contact, taking the opportunity to try another approach with my steak. I stabbed it deeply in the middle with my fork, then flipped the entire thing over, and resumed sawing on the other side.

Just like I instinctively picked up on the etiquette of not ordering a tall glass of milk on a hot date, I knew it was not cool to be
a girl who picked at her food. You wanted to be a fun date who ate
like a normal person. When Kyle got up to go the bathroom, I at-
tacked the meat, plunging the tip of the knife through the center of
it, wedging my fork in the cavity, and attempting to carve out a
chunk by rotating the knife in a counterclockwise motion. I had to
eat as much as possible while he was gone. I plunged my finger into
the hole, ripped the steak in half, and then leaned forward so that
my hair fell in my face. Quickly, I picked up a hunk and tore at it
with my teeth, gnawing off an enormous piece. It was then that
Kyle came back.

"Wow," he said, glancing around the restaurant before sitting
back down. "Do you need some help cutting that?"

I nodded and pushed my plate toward him. We sat in silence as
he calmly sliced my entire steak into manageable bite-sized pieces
and set it back down in front of me.

After splitting an enormous chocolate dessert called a bomb,
or an avalanche, or an orgasm, whatever that was, he asked me if I
wanted to go back to his place. He lived with his grandparents who
went to bed early, so I was hoping that meant we might be able to
make out a little. I didn't want to throw his sense of propriety out of
balance, but I thought he'd be surprised that a freshman was such a
good kisser.

He pulled the car into the circular driveway and quickly
hopped out to open my door for me. We snuck into the house, leav-

ing all the lights off, as he led me into the darkened living room and sat me down on the brown, pleather sofa. He disappeared and came back with two glasses of Tang on a serving tray. It was then that he asked for a kiss. I was thrilled by his gallantry. He was definitely not like all the other boys.

He leaned in to kiss me. *This is the greatest night of my life,* I thought as his angular, smooth-shaven face came toward me. In that moment, I imagined our future together, exchanging Christmas presents, going to his senior prom together, and spending the summer frequenting the best restaurants around—Chili's, TGI Fridays, you name it. We would dip curly fries in ranch dressing all the way across the valley. Then he would go off to college, a military academy which would enforce rules of strict gender separation and therefore deprive him of female contact for four years. Pining away for his girl back home, he'd write me long letters on cold nights from the Hudson River fortress. I had seen *An Officer and a Gentleman.* Love would lift us up where we belonged. I let my imagination run wild in those thirty seconds that we were making out before he whispered something in my ear.

Huh? What was that he just said? I stopped for a second because I must not have heard him correctly. It almost sounded like he had said, "I want you to suck my dick." Strange. I ignored it and kept kissing him, but about ten seconds later, his mouth went to my ear and again he said, a little louder, "Suck my dick." Finally, when he said it a third time, I decided to deal with the situation head on. Instead of reluctantly acquiescing or spouting off some Girl Power quip that wouldn't be invented for another ten years, I leaned back on the couch and looked at him with a twinge of disappointment. "Aw, man," I said. "I really don't want to suck your dick right now. I'm totally sorry, but it just seems weird."

We got in the car, and he drove me home. His ski handle stick shift just looked stupid now. My parents were waiting up for me, all excited to hear how my big date went. I offered them the highlights—the steak incident, the chocolate dessert, and the Tang. When I went to my room, I saw that my mom had placed the bud vase on my bedside table next to the bouquet of roses from the night before—souvenirs of my big debutante weekend that she'd later ask if I wanted to press into a scrapbook. Um, no.

So that was it for Kyle and me. I felt lame for letting him spend fifty bucks on that dinner, although I have learned in the intervening years that it wasn't just him. Apparently the whole world wants its dick sucked by a fourteen-year-old girl.

Kyle moved on to date a girl from another school named Trisha, whom he actually ended up marrying after he graduated from West Point. I was out of the country at the time, but my parents said it was a large, expensive wedding at a military base that involved a lot of people in uniform and the two of them passing under some kind of canopy formed by rifles. I think shots were fired. It wasn't even a year before Kyle found out that Trisha was cheating on him with an eighteen-year-old housepainter and had been since before they were engaged. They divorced immediately, probably before all three hundred guests at the ceremony had even sent in their presents. My parents, who purchased a nice pizza stone for them from Williams-Sonoma, were shocked, but all they did was shake their heads and say, "What a shame." My parents would never say a mean thing about anyone.

High school turned out fine for me. I ended up going out with a skinny, cross-country runner who had the amazing ability to rip off farts at will and once bought me a toilet seat for Christmas. So that was cool. I was happy. But because of that one date, I learned a valuable lesson early in life. At fourteen, I already began avoiding people who were suave, classically attractive, and socially adept. It's kind of a cliché that all the interesting people you meet as adults claim to have been big losers in high school, but when I look at my friends and heroes now, I see a bunch of teens who were nose-in-the-book intellectuals, *Dungeons & Dragons* nerds, angry punks, chess prodigies, band geeks, sensitive Goths, and confused queers. I wasn't an outcast at all in high school, but I did blow my chance for ever winning another crown because I couldn't hack the pressure of being popular. My adolescent obsession of ferreting out phonies stuck with me. So now I keep away from smooth talkers. And I stay out of the sun.

④ NUNS IN TROUBLE

The weekend before I started college, I made fifty bucks working as a hair model for a Beverly Hills salon. There was a big industry trade show in town, and they were recruiting a batch of girls who wouldn't mind giving the team of hair professionals free rein with color and style. Clutching their portfolios, not too many of the aspiring models who showed up were game, but I told the Italian gentleman in charge that I didn't care what they did to me. I dared them to come up with a hairdo worse than the one I was currently sporting.

Two months earlier, on the eve of embarking on a postgraduation trip to Europe with Amy, I had shaved off most of my hair with my brother Chris's electric clippers. Then I just let it grow. My appointed hairdresser, a man with a flowing, highlighted mane who went by the name of Bruce Wayne (but who was neither a

Batman fan nor that guy who does the interviews in *Vanity Fair*) cringed.

"Do you remember those monkey dolls? The Monchichi?" he asked, eyeing my fuzzy, mouse-brown halo. "It looks like a cross between one of those and a newt."

The Gothy assistant with magenta-rimmed eyes stepped up. "I get the Monchichi thing," she said, running her fingers over my scalp. "But how does it look like a newt?"

"Oh," Bruce said as an afterthought, blowing a stray hair out of his eye. "Just her face. There's something a little newt-like in the face."

I checked myself out in the mirror. My resemblance to rats, birds, and fish had all been noted before, but I had never been referred to as anything from the reptilian or amphibian world. I remembered a long rant my biology teacher once made about the heartless, militaristic nature of the reptilian brain. Relief washed over me. Bruce didn't imply I had the *brain* of a reptile; he only said I looked like one.

I let them bleach my hair out, chop it into chunky vertical swatches, tart me up with *Blade Runner* makeup, and parade me across a runway in a see-through dress. When I got in my 1979 Honda Accord to drive home, I took a good look at myself in the rearview mirror. My eyes were covered with a wide bandit's mask of black eyeshadow, and my lips were lined in orange and filled in with charcoal lipstick. The ghostly powder on my face stopped right at my jawline, creating a line between my face and my neck that I knew was definitely a fashion "don't." I looked as bad as when I came in, just a different kind of bad—bad in that faux punk rock way.

This seemed like a crime to me. Somewhere out in the world were real punk rockers. I had read about them in magazines and had even been to a few shows with them. I may have listened to a lot of the same music they did, but I knew I would never be punk. I was an upper-middle-class girl on my way to college who had just spent three hours in a discount suite at the Santa Clara Doubletree Hotel with a team of stylists from a salon on Rodeo Drive. I cruised through the Saturday afternoon traffic, wondering how this new look would affect my life. I was embarrassed to look like such a poseur, like the kids at my high school who ripped their jeans on purpose and then safety pinned them together. By the time I coasted through the drive-through at Taco Bravo, trying to be extra friendly when ordering my burrito to counteract my menacing appearance, I had an epiphany: This hair made perfect sense on me. If anyone cared, it announced that I was the kind of person who would commit any fashion crime that would make me fifty dollars richer.

With that important existential crisis resolved, I returned home to find my mom in my bedroom, helping me pack up for my freshman dorm at UC—Santa Cruz. Upon seeing me, she cried real tears. My mom wept easily anyway, welling up any time we mentioned Apples, our deceased dog who had suffered from a horrible flea allergy that made him chew all the hair off of his ass. She could also be moved to tears by such cultural touchstones as Vivaldi,

Spielberg, and Oprah, but I wasn't ready for the "going away to college" sob just yet. My school was only a half hour drive away. I still had three nights left in the house. Why was she getting so emotional?

"I'm sorry," she said, hugging me gently. "You probably already know this, but you look very scary right now."

"But look at this," I said, breaking out my cash-filled envelope. "I got paid fifty bucks for this!"

"Why?" she asked, going back to winding toilet paper around my collection of glass and ceramic mouse figurines. "Why do you need fifty dollars so badly?"

She should have known better. It wasn't about the money. I had been scanning the classifieds in the *San Jose Mercury News* at the kitchen table for years, answering ads for vitamin salespeople and seltzer water distributors, not quite sure of the most effective way to break out of the monotony of high school. I guess some kids turned to Rumplemintz or whipped cream canisters to escape. I just wanted to be the world's youngest taxi dispatcher or hotel concierge. At eighteen, I had already held part-time jobs catering, selling tickets to the firefighters' rodeo, and working as an office assistant in a plastic surgery suite. A job, any job, was what made you real in the world. College sounded okay, but I had to be honest with myself. I was only going to college because where I came from, it was the same as going to church or the orthodontist. You just went. You asked questions later, if ever.

My entire first year in college, I refrained from seeking out work because I was living on campus, and most of the available jobs were in the library or dining hall. I was already surrounded by a community of eighteen year olds who were learning about Hegel's Theory of the Modern State for the first time; I didn't want to have to slice up carrot coins with them as well. I would hold out for something more meaningful, like a position at a telephone solicitation bank or a job on the downtown assembly line that manufactured the plastic bins that stored bulk foods at the supermarket. I'd spent most of my savings on my trip the previous summer, but I still had enough money to tide me over until the end of the school year.

The afternoon after my last final of the year, I hit the streets. All I wanted that summer was to work. I was living in a beach town, a place lousy with surfers, tourists, and party kids, but I might as well have been landlocked at a religious work camp for teens with discipline problems. The problem was I didn't drink. I didn't do drugs. I only wanted to fill my hours with a minimum-wage job. Now that the rate had just been raised from $3.35 to $4.25 an hour, I could clear almost a hundred and fifty dollars a week *after* taxes!

The first place to call me back was a bakery that needed a counter person. Named after the owner, Emily's Bakery had a sign over the front door that read, "Relax: You Have Plenty of Time." It would be a summer of good vibes and baked goods. I liked the idea of a bakery. It seemed so honest and wholesome.

I worked full-time through the summer, and when school started again, I cut my hours back to about fifteen a week. But soon enough, I was signing up for extra shifts and covering for people who were sick. Some days I would wake up, ride my bike over to help with the morning rush, go to classes for a few hours, and then return to help close. Dealing with customers definitely kept me busy, but I especially enjoyed my side work, which included scooping out hundreds of balls of dough with an ice cream scoop or individually wrapping dozens and dozens of cookies in cellophane. At school, there was too much talking and thinking going on. What I loved was a good rote task.

A couple of months into the school year, I was up to working twenty hours a week and learning to bake. I was helping the master baker shape breads, learning about the vagaries of sourdough starter, making muffin batters, and seasoning croutons. I still planned on graduating from college, but I decided I wanted to become a pastry chef. My boyfriend Morgan worked at a semifancy restaurant downtown as a waiter, and as soon as a position opened up there, where I could learn how to make tarts and crème brûlée, I took it.

Over Christmas break, Morgan went to Hawaii with his family for two weeks, and I picked up extra shifts at the restaurant. I was working almost forty hours a week and feeling exhausted. Something was wrong with me. I could barely get out of bed in the morning and would crash out shortly after getting home. I went to the restaurant every day to do prep work for the holiday onslaught, but I was tired and sluggish. Even my old pals, caffeine and sugar, which I would usually ride like a roller coaster all day long, had no effect.

One afternoon, as I was arranging crushed pistachios on a rosewater torte, a hostess named Roberta came into the kitchen to graze on leftover desserts. Like many other part-time service industry workers in the town of Santa Cruz, Roberta had psychic powers. She leaned against the table, quietly watching me work. When she finished her coconut cream pie, she set her dish down and said, "Are you someone's mother?" That's when it dawned on me. I was pregnant. Drag.

The good thing about having an unwanted pregnancy in a liberal hippie town is that everyone understands how you're feeling, even if they don't. There's no need to be ashamed or embarrassed because, in a community known for its inclination to "over-share," chances are you've heard enough horror stories about molestation, abuse, and addiction to consider yourself pretty lucky. I saw the problem as financial and logistical.

I was twenty years old. Of course I wasn't going to have a baby. So I did what every other young woman who has recently learned about the of tyranny of Western medicine does: I drank a shitload of pennyroyal tea. When eighteen straight hours of that didn't induce the hoped-for spontaneous abortion, I called the clinic. Three hundred bucks. Too bad I only had half that.

When Morgan and I finally spoke, while he was drinking a chi-chi at a resort on Maui, he felt terrible and wanted me to wait for him to return. But there was no way. I couldn't wait around being pregnant for a whole extra week. He said he would give me half the money when he got back, but I had to come up with the full amount before then.

Of course, I *could* have told my parents the whole story and asked them for money. They would have supported me and administered only a mild lecture. But I had a paycheck coming in a few days, and beyond that, I only needed seventy-five more dollars. It seemed like too much trouble to go through for only seventy-five bucks. There was also something distasteful about going through a scene that had been played out so often in books, movies, and television: *Daughter tells her parents about the unwanted pregnancy. An awkward silence follows as the parents exchange looks. Daughter hangs her head in shame, a woman in some ways and yet still a child. Dad nods at mom, who moves in for the hug. Dad joins in, and they stand there in the living room, the three of them, lit by the sparkling Christmas tree lights and the warm glow of the fireplace.* Oh, man. I needed to make some money quick. I got the newspaper and turned to the classifieds.

It helped that it was Christmastime because there was a lot of seasonal work, although at that moment, I couldn't imagine loading UPS trucks or wrangling dogs at the Citizen Canine boarding kennel. I called a number that was advertising for workers at a holiday party.

"Catholic Charities, Sister Dorothy speaking."

No. Way. My cheeks flushed. Even I was embarrassed by the ham-handed irony. I was pregnant, seeking a way to fund my abortion, and I was on the phone with Sister Dorothy at the Catholic Charities office.

It sounded like I had just interrupted her snack break. Her mouth seemed to be full of crackers, although I imagined them as communion wafers. I always wondered if priests and nuns were allowed to eat those whenever they wanted, spreading them with a nutty cheese log or dipping them in guacamole.

"Hi! My name is Beth, and I'm calling about the ad in the paper for the party."

"Oh, yes! Yes!" she said. I heard the distinct sound of her popping open a soda can. "We're looking for some girls to help with our benefit party next Friday night, our big Christmas fundraiser. The party goes from six until midnight, and we'll pay you fifty dollars."

"Okay, that sounds great!" Fifty bucks. I was so relieved. "I can totally do it."

"Not so fast," she said. "Can I ask you a question, Dot?"

"Oh, it's Beth," I said.

"Sorry, Betty. Listen, how tall are you?"

"Um, five-seven or five-eight."

"Oooh! Perfect!" she said. "We like the girls to be tall!" She covered the mouthpiece with her hand and stage-whispered, "Says she's five-eight!"

That set off a few bells. From all my years of answering classifieds, I was always wary of a job that specified body type, hair color, or an "open-minded attitude." There were a lot of people looking for models and actresses for their "art projects."

"Okay, wait." I said. "What am I going to be doing exactly?"

"Well, you just have to help sell raffle tickets," she said.

"All right. No problem," I said. "So I just show up at six?"

"No, no. Don't get ahead of yourself. Let me ask you this. You a pretty slim girl, Betty? On the slender side of things?" I heard her pop another wafer into her mouth.

"Yeah, I guess so," I said.

"Great! And how old are you?"

"I'm twenty."

It sounded like she accidentally sat on a cat.

"Perfect! Why don't you come down this Wednesday at two, and we can meet you and get everything all settled."

We hung up, and I imagined her leaning over to the other sisters in the TV lounge saying, "We've got a live one!"

The pregnancy had me feeling nearly narcoleptic. I would take a shower, decide to "rest my eyes" for a bit, and wake up three hours later, naked with a towel wrapped around my head. On my day off, I wandered around the house in a daze, falling asleep at the kitchen counter with my chin resting in my hand or my face in the laundry basket. I just needed to get through this week.

After working at the bakery all morning, I got off my shift and drove over to the Catholic Charities office. I was wearing jeans covered in melted chocolate from dipping hundreds of strawberries and a T-shirt displaying a cartoon hippie leaning out of a souped-up van. It said, "Gas, Grass or Ass. Nobody rides for free." I rummaged through my car for something to cover it up and found a cardigan laced with dipstick marks from using it to check my oil.

About eight girls were standing outside when I pulled up.

Clutching their portfolios, they reminded me of the girls from the hair show. Most of them were my age, although there was one older woman in a lavender sweater dress who looked like she had just been to hell and back. While the other girls compared head shots and complimented one another on their most photogenic features (*You have killer eyebrows! Look at your cheekbones in this one!*), she scowled from beneath her yellow rat's nest of bangs, smoking a skinny lady cigarette and grinding the heel of her white pump into a flattened Chicken McNuggets box on the ground.

A couple of minutes later, two sisters came scurrying up the path. I loved the modern nun outfits with the navy blue A-lined skirts and cardigan sweaters. The skinny one waved and introduced herself as Sister Helen. She looked about thirty and was wearing men's black dress socks with her outfit, like the kind my dad wore to work every day. The other nun was Sister Dorothy, the wafer popper who had answered my phone call.

"Okay, girls! We are so sorry for making you wait!" she said, clapping her hands together and rocking back and forth on the rubber soles of her Famolares.

Once inside the office, we signed our names on a clipboard and were called one by one to the back of the room. The nuns seemed to be running their own talent agency. Awaiting my turn, I picked up a copy of the church bulletin and tried not to fall asleep. The only photo in it was of the previous week's canned food drive. Just a bunch of cans piled in a box that had a shaky little halo drawn on it.

When my name was called, I approached the table where Sister Dorothy, Sister Helen, and an older nun were seated.

"This is Sister Theresa," Sister Dorothy said. "If your uniform needs altering, she's the one who's going to do it. She made them all by herself."

Sister Theresa looked me over and declared, "You look like a six, but you could be an eight. I bet you're an eight on the bottom."

She handed me a pair of gray shorts and a matching bellboy-style jacket. I looked around for a place to change.

"You can change right here," Sister Dorothy said. "Let's see if you fit the suit."

I took off my chocolate-splattered jeans in front of them and slipped on the shorts. They were pretty short, like hot pants, but made out of a lightweight wool.

"Excellent," Sister Helen said, circling me. "Now we'll want you to wear heels with this. Do you have some black heels?"

"Yeah," I said, even though I didn't. I knew I could get some cheap at a thrift store or borrow a pair from a roommate. I had just lied to a nun.

The outfit had sort of a 1940s cigarette girl look to it. It came with a little square hat with a chin strap. It was saucy yet classy, but astonishingly not like anything I would really expect from the Catholic Church. I guess I did know that, historically speaking, they did have a thing for uniforms.

They told me all I had to do was show up at the ballroom of

the Coconut Grove, a large waterfront hotel, on Friday evening at 5:30 P.M. And there was one more thing: "I'm going to take up those shorts for you," Sister Theresa said, pinning the hem a little. "I think they could be a little shorter."

On Friday evening, fresh off my shift at the bakery, I showed up at the ballroom and was directed to the dressing room. Sister Dorothy was there, but Sister Helen and Sister Theresa had been replaced by two other nuns. The three other girls hired for the job had already arrived in full makeup. Two of them, Stacy and Tracy, were friends. And then there was Tamarind.

"Excuse me, Tamarind?" Sister Dorothy was saying. "Maybe you could go a little easy on the eyeliner tonight? If you wouldn't mind?"

Poor Tamarind. Her mother had already given her the name of a stripper, and now the nuns were hassling her.

Tamarind smiled a completely fake smile, and as soon as the nun turned around, she yanked her hand back and forth in front of her mouth like she was giving a blow job. Stacy and Tracy laughed.

I had some respect for the nuns. One of my great aunts was the Mother Superior of a Carmelite monastery. She had been living with the Discalced Nuns of the Carmel at the Monastery of Mary, Mother of Grace in Lafayette, Louisiana, for the past forty years. The Carmelites were a cloistered sect who took a vow of silence, engaged in profound prayer throughout their lives, grew their own food, sewed liturgical vestments, and even weaved their own sandals. I told this to Sister Dorothy.

"Well, I suppose that's one way to do it," she remarked, flipping on a mini-TV and leaning back in her chair.

Sister Margaret, a young, nervous-looking nun who barely opened her mouth when she spoke, gave us the run-down. The way she refused to make eye contact with us, rapidly shifting her focus around, made her look like a criminal in a film noir.

"There are eight Christmas trees lining the ballroom, okay? Each tree has its own theme. I can't remember all of them, but one has a beach theme and one has to do with winter. One raffle ticket gets you in the drawing for one of the trees. One ticket. One tree. The tickets are five dollars a piece, but we have a deal. We have a deal, see where you can get five for twenty dollars, all right? One for five. Five for twenty."

I looked over at Stacy and Tracy, who were pretty much laughing openly in Sister Margaret's face. Tamarind was focusing very hard on the small port wine stain on her cheek.

"The buyer's going to hand you money," she continued. "Ones, fives, tens, twenties, it could be any type of bill. You put the money in your tray." She motioned over to a set of wooden trays with leather straps affixed to them. The cigarette girl look was complete.

"Can I ask a question?" Tracy or Stacy asked. "How do we know which tree they're buying for? Or does it matter?"

Sister Margaret forced a sarcastic chuckle. "Does it *matter*? Does it matter which tree?" She swung her head around, scanning the room. "Yes, I would say it matters a whole lot because if you want Surfin' Safari, the tree with the Hawaiian vacation package underneath it, you're going to be miffed if your ticket doesn't go in the right can."

"Can?" I asked. "What can?"

She suddenly stopped shifting her eyes and looked us all over, one at a time. "Follow me."

She led us over to a table where Sister Dorothy and the other nun were arranging coffee cans and raffle tickets.

"Each time you sell a ticket, you write down which tree the person is buying the ticket for. The trees are clearly marked. Tree one is Rock-and-Roll Tree, tree two is Pink Christmas Tree, tree three is Surfin' Safari Tree, et cetera. When you bring the tickets back to us, we will look at the back of the ticket and drop them into the correct can. At the end of the night, there will be eight separate drawings for the eight trees."

Sister Dorothy interrupted: "Father Paul says they're opening the doors!"

There was a flurry of activity as Sister Margaret placed the trays around our necks, and the silent nun tore off a strip of tickets for each of us. As I walked onto the floor, the ballroom doors were flung open, and a herd of the county's finest Catholic senior citizenry came stampeding in. The men were in tuxes, the women in floor-length gowns, and the nuns—beside themselves entirely.

"Oh, look at that sequined number!" Sister Dolores gasped

loudly, standing in the doorway to the back room with her hands on her hips. "Only Kitty could pull that off!"

I roamed the floor in my slutty Salvation Army stilettos, which were a half size too small but had nice little gold caps on the toes.

Scoping out the trees, I quickly identified the Surfin' Safari Tree, with the surfboard and poolside lounge chair underneath, and the Winter Wonderland Tree with its skis, sleigh, and snowman made of L.L. Bean Fair Isle sweaters. Many of the themes were unclear to me. One tree appeared to be Elvis-inspired. Another one seemed to be all about the color pink. Under its pink-flocked branches was a tutu with tickets to *The Nutcracker*, a dozen roses with a gift certificate for a year's worth of monthly deliveries, and— seemingly at odds with the event's target market—tickets to a Pink Floyd night at the Laserium in San Jose.

As soon as the guests found their tables, they were completely engrossed in the raffle until dinner was served. People were buying ten or twenty tickets at a time. One man gave me a hundred dollar bill, and as soon as I counted out fifteen tickets, he told me to keep the change. I desperately wanted to, but I had no pockets in my uniform and wouldn't dare bring the extra bills back to the Nun Room and stuff them in my backpack.

Within fifteen minutes, my tray was overflowing with money. There were no compartments to organize the cash or separate the purchased tickets from the ones I still had to sell. If I walked too fast across the room, everything would fly out onto the floor.

"Let me see you do that again!" joked one gin-blossomed grandpa-type as I bent over to retrieve a flyaway bill.

I smiled and shuffled over to Sister Dolores, who was busy broadcasting the evening's highlights to the other two sisters. "Mr. Chavez apparently told Father Paul that he wants to help out with the new rectory," she was saying excitedly.

"Hi," I said, gesturing to my tray. "I've got a lot of money and tickets here."

Sister Margaret hurried over and plunged both of her hands into the tray, pulling fistfuls of bills and tickets out and piling them on the table. The silent nun handed me another curled strip of tickets, and they went about organizing and sorting.

"Can I have a few dollars for change?" I asked. "Just some ones and fives would be great."

I watched Sister Dorothy reach into the pile of money and, without counting it, drop a handful in my tray. "You're doing good!" she said. "Get out there, and come back with more!"

On my way back out to the floor, Tamarind came wobbling in, a mountain of money in her tray. "These people are sooooo wrong," she said under her breath as the nuns rushed in and unloaded her stash.

This time, I decided to try a new tactic. Instead of roaming around the ballroom, I was going to let people come to me. I was with child for God's sake. I leaned against a pole toward the back of the room by the bar and waited for the raffle enthusiasts to find me.

Across the room, I could see Stacy and Tracy table surfing for aban-doned cocktails.

About twenty minutes later, people were being seated for din-ner. It seemed like a good time to take a break. My tray could have used a dumping, but I decided to go to the bathroom and stave off another nun encounter for at least five more minutes. I walked down a long corridor, through a door, and emerged in a fluorescent lit hallway. There must be a closer bathroom, I thought as I took an-other turn into another hotel hallway, until finally reaching a land-ing with a sign. In the bathroom, I took the tray from around my neck and placed it on the counter. What if somebody came in? I couldn't leave all this money out here. It was at least four hundred bucks. I slipped the tray back on and went into a stall, somehow managing to shimmy my shorts down and sit with the tray of money in my lap. I'd never had a tray of cash in my lap before, let alone while peeing.

It suddenly occurred to me that this was completely unac-counted for cash. I flashed back to the nuns' pell-mell handling of the entire affair. They had no idea how many tickets were even be-ing sold or how much money each girl returned with. If I took a few bucks, they would never know the difference. And if they did sus-pect that someone was ripping them off, they'd never suspect me—the one with the aunt who was the Mother Superior of the Carmelite monastery. However, I was probably the only one who was also pregnant with an abortion scheduled for the following week. I immediately saw the cracks in my own theory.

When I went back out to empty my tray before dinner ended, things had devolved even further. The silent nun was asleep in her chair. Sister Dolores and Sister Margaret were devouring lamb shanks on a far couch. Stacey and Tracy looked wasted. And Tamarind was nowhere to be found. Sister Theresa said her tray had been spotted at a corner table, still full of cash and tickets. This operation is a joke, I thought, as my hat slid down over my eyes. I was shocked by the level of confusion and chaos, yet I had to admit, I fit in perfectly. What would this Catholic charity ball have been without me? I was sure everyone here had their own dirty secrets, but I had to believe mine was the best to get through the night.

When the big band started to play, there was a whole new rush for the raffle. Couples would dance for a few songs and then wander over to buy more tickets. Some of them were too drunk to remember how many they'd already bought. One woman told me she stole fifty dollars out of her husband's wallet because he had cut her off for the night. I kept my eye out for the man who tried to tip me. This time I would take the money, I told myself, even if it meant stashing it under the tanbark of a rubber tree plant until the evening was over.

I'd soon accumulated yet another wad of bills. With everybody else either doing shots with the bartender or totally MIA, most of the business was coming through me. I started to get self-righteous. If these people—these drunk Catholics and their incompetent employees—knew about my situation, they would call me a sinner. Some of them might even want to open their hearts and forgive me for my supposed evildoing. Looking at them started to give me the creeps.

The evening was finally winding down. The raffle was fifteen minutes away, when I made one last trip to the bathroom. I had taken off my shoes and was padding along the carpet, listening to the piped-in music. It sounded like a Muzak version of ELO's "Don't Bring Me Down" to a bossa nova beat. I felt delirious. I set my shoes and hat on the counter, went into the stall with my tray, and looked at the money. As I sat there peeing, my eyes at half mast, I unfastened the brass buttons on my coat, picked out two twenty dollar bills and tucked them into my black bustier. The only other thing I'd ever stolen before was a magazine when I was in the third grade because it had pictures of Robert Blake as Baretta. Why was I doing this? And why was I wearing a black bustier? Where did I get this thing anyway? Is this ELO? Or is it "Does Your Mother Know?" by ABBA? Could I go home now? I had to be at work the next day at 7:00 A.M.

I walked back out through the ballroom to the Nun Room. The raffle was about to start, and I still had to sort my new tickets in the corresponding coffee cans. Sister Dorothy took the money out of my tray, counted out fifty dollars, and handed the bills to me. Then she invited me to stick around for the big moment, in case I was curious to see who was going to walk with Surfin' Safari.

I changed back into my clothes, slipped out of the building, and headed for my car. It was cold for Santa Cruz, and the wind was coming up off the water in short, sharp gusts. On the way home, I got confused and forgot that I had moved a few months earlier to the other side of town. God, what was wrong me? Women got pregnant by mistake all the time. I made a quick U-turn in the middle of the street. That's when I felt a corner of the stolen bills digging into my skin. My money—I had forgotten it was there. Everything would be okay now, I thought, all thanks to the nuns—those unwitting sisters of mercy.

⑤ MY WAY OR THE BI-WAY

When I went away to college at UC—Santa Cruz, all it took was reading some pamphlets on how industrial hemp was a viable natural resource and fountainhead of sustainable energy for me to decide that I was probably bisexual. I'd never been attracted to girls before or anything, but suddenly learning about things like illegal strawberry-harvesting practices, the etymology of the word "history," and Citizens in Solidarity with the People of El Salvador, along with a teeming host of other hot button issues, pointed me in the same direction. Obviously, a truly open-minded person would love men and women equally, and she would also have a compost pile in her backyard. Gender is fluid. Pesticides are bad. Eve was framed. Green tea kills free radicals. Sex is fun. The world is made of fractals. Whatever. All I knew was that I believed Anita,

Tawana, and that as a liberal, freethinking individual, I had to be bisexual. It all made sense in the hazy redwood forest of my mind.

By far the most powerful of my unfounded revelations was that this didn't apply only to me. *The entire world is bisexual,* I'd decided while spooning an overpriced, soybean-based, frozen dairy substitute dessert into my mouth. It's just that most people are too uptight to ever realize it. We are all people of the earth, I tried to tell myself, rallying, turning a blind eye to the fact that there were very few people of the earth with whom I wanted to spend time naked. That the world comprises a pansexual populace seemed as obvious as the injustice of a slaughterhouse full of beakless chickens at a factory farm and, frankly, just about as sexy.

Although still a virgin when I entered college, I had considered myself a sexual pioneer since youth. As Mrs. Hilding, my fifth-grade teacher, so discreetly put it at a parent/teacher conference with my mother, "Spring came early for Beth this year." And I wasn't into any of the baby games like Spin the Bottle or Three Minutes in the Closet either. Decked out in my tight Sassoon jeans tucked into my brown pleather boots, my hair perfectly feathered, I was ready for some hot behind-the-bushes action. I always made the first move, whether I was commandeering the handball court on the playground or seeking out boys who lingered at the haunted house at the amusement park. Skateboarders, BMXers, runty class clowns—I loved the tough guys.

In junior high, back before the Santa Clara Valley was called Silicon Valley, when it was still nicknamed the Valley of Hearts'

Delight, I'd meet my boyfriends in plum orchards by the library or the country club's swimming pool, and we'd do nearly everything except "it." By high school, my boyfriend's parents would be passed out drunk in the next room of their ranch house, and I'd be forced to safeguard my technical virginity against some hormonally super-charged eighteen-year-old who'd already had sex with previous girl-friends and now had the misfortune to be dating a World Series cock tease. To this day, I'm not sure what forces were at work that allowed me to enjoy cunnilingus as a fourteen-year-old.

All I can say is that upon scanning my former high school crowd while home during Christmas break during my freshman year of college, I was astounded at my foresight not to have had sexual intercourse with anyone in that student body. Those boys, now frat brothers draining beers at the bar before cutting loose to "Funky-town" on the dance floor, didn't have shit on me.

At Santa Cruz, everyone loved to joke about LUGs, those "les-bians until graduation" (later called "hasbians"). This was supposed to be a very serious insult, like you were a "fake" queer, just pretending you were gay until you went out in the real world and couldn't face the homophobia. But I was different. I was not enchanted with some Sapphic vision of womyn loving womyn, nor was I going to orgies, reading Anaïs Nin, having threesomes with my boyfriend, having threesomes with my girlfriend's boyfriend, or making out with other former straight girls at the kegger. I believed what I had was truly a philosophy: an open-minded bisexual, virgin's philosophy. This sounds like a punch line, but I was serious. I may have joined the women's rugby team and been flattered when they attempted to lure me to hot tub parties during the full moon on a deck overlooking the Pacific, but I didn't accept their open invitations. Those rugby players were just like the senior football players at my high school as far as I was concerned, only more butch. They were a tight-knit club of swaggering jocks, and I wasn't going to let them prey on me.

Although I eventually "did it" with my environmentally conscious, Mendocino mountain-biker boyfriend, to the appropriate collegiate sound track of Bob Marley's "Uprising," I made it all the way through college without ever kissing a girl—a remarkable feat considering the statistics. The whole time I assumed that I just hadn't found the right girl yet. I wasn't into being bisexual because I thought it was cool. Otherwise, I might have told someone or at least acted on it once or twice to get people off my back. I'd decided that bisexuality was simply a fact of nature, hardly different from a pile of dirt or a mound of clover.

After graduation, I moved to a small railroad flat in the Mission District of San Francisco. I was living with my boyfriend, a quiet artist whose dad had been a teen heartthrob from a 1960s TV show. Every time we went somewhere with Morgan's dad, people thought they recognized him—but not from TV. He had so often played roles like a rapist on *CHiPs* and a retarded janitor on *Charlie's Angels* that people were familiar enough with his face to think they went to high school with him or used to serve him boilermakers at a bar in Indianapolis. He was utterly recognizable to a huge percentage of the American population, but no one knew why.

I was working as a baker at the time, waking up at 3:30 A.M. and cranking out bread and desserts until noon. I'd clock out, totally exhausted, go home for some lunch, a little wine, and a nap. Except I always drank a lot of wine and would sleep well past my self-imposed, two-hour limit. I was miserable. What was there at work to get remotely excited about? The head chef was potentially alluring in his checkered pants and white coat until he stopped by on his day off wearing a tie-dye shirt and open-toed shoes on his way to a Phish concert. I guess that's why there are uniform fetishists. You can just embrace the idea of The Cop or The Doctor without having to think about The Mock Turtleneck or The Elastic Waistband. But wait—what about Bernice the other baker? She was always vaguely flirting with me. Because she was something of an old-school lesbian, the fact that I was acquainted with the music of Joan Armatrading and wore formless T-shirts and Doc Martens got a lot more mileage with her than it might have with someone my own age. We'd reload the flour bins together, and I'd ask her about her former career in the army. I'd never met anyone who got paid to boss people around in Guam.

One morning after we'd finished coating the cheese buns with egg wash, she straight up asked me out, as in, "Let's go out after work today." I definitely liked her and thought she was cool, but my dissatisfaction with my personal life made me indifferent to whether we wound up at a baseball game or in Reno. I would have gone anywhere. Instead, we just drove her Jeep down to the local lesbian bar and had a few beers, as if we both knew a little afternoon drinking would help us sort this all out. Emboldened by Anchor Steam on an empty stomach, I convinced her that we should go downstairs to a place called The Gauntlet and get something pierced. The wild descent into a debauched marathon of drinking and urban primitivism ended when I got a small ring in the cartilage of my upper ear, and she pierced her earlobes for the first time.

Our date was over by 6:00 P.M., just in time for Bernice to get to bed for her 3:00 A.M. shift the next morning. Not exactly a steamy time with the Aerobisex Girls. As she pulled up next to my truck to drop me off, I decided to be bold. I'd never not kissed on a first date—why start now? I leaned over the stick shift, completely prepared to launch into a full-on make out session. There was no way I was doing any half-assed kissing my first time with a girl. I grabbed her by the back of her poodle perm and went for it. Her breath was warm and beery, her face a lot softer than I had imagined, but after a minute or two, I retreated. The only thing I felt was a little sore around the ear as pus started to seep out. Damn. I drove back to my apartment wondering why an adventurous, freewheeling bisexual like me wasn't remotely turned on.

I soldiered onward, deciding to satisfy my urge for lady sex with some erotic videos from the local, women-run, workers' cooperative sex emporium. Even though this whole idea of "sex positivity" had been drilled into me for years, when it came right down to it, I was actually a little embarrassed to stroll into Good Vibrations in my baking uniform at 2:00 P.M. to rent porn. I realized that the employees, with their open, friendly faces and early 1990s urban sexual sophistication, had been trained to love perverts of every stripe, but I still tried to select something that didn't look too explicit—as if I was doing research about something lesbian-related, but not totally lesbionic. As fate would have it, I wound up with a hilarious low-budget video of women stripping for one another in cramped studio apartments and poorly lit rec rooms to a muffled sound track of folk tunes. I think it was called Sister Strip. I passed out with my chef's coat on and my undies on the floor, unfulfilled.

Perhaps what I needed was a gal pal. All this making eyes with the telephone repairwoman and embarrassing innuendo with the FedEx dyke was getting me nowhere. Could I just be the Madonna to some fabulous Sandra Bernhard character? You know, we could wow the crowds at the AIDS dance-a-thon in our cutoff shorts and spangly bra tops. Launching into deep tongue kisses and irreverent ass grabbing, suspended in a go-go cage high above the crowds, we would crack ourselves up as we showed those unimaginative straight people what was what. Or maybe I'd rather become Sandra, except less difficult and without the fixation on supermodels? Or did San Francisco have its own Ingrid Casares or whatever that lady's name is with the nightclubs in South Beach? The one who also went out with Madonna? These ladies made being a girl who was into girls look like a nonstop game of Candyland. Where was I going wrong?

It was only through the power of positive thinking that I finally got some action. The kickoff took place while I was fast asleep on the couch at a friend's house, which I suppose is sort of like being molested, if you want to get technical. I woke up to find this gorgeous, Scottish girl—a mix of male, female, and otherworldliness whom I had nicknamed the Androgynaut earlier at the bar—leaning over me, kissing my neck, whispering in my ear, her hands on my lower back and in my hair. This might be somebody I could get into, I thought for about a minute, until I came to and remembered that she was the new girlfriend of a friend of mine—a friend who also happened to be asleep in the next room.

About a year later, I was in Seattle to perform at Lollapalooza. Like a lot of fledgling writers, I had discovered the strange miracle of the "open mic poetry night" and had been reading my stuff in bars and cafés around town. They were just half-baked rants about yuppies or short stories about riding the bus, but I realized something: Public speaking was supposed to be many people's worst fear, but it didn't even make my top five.

MY TOP FIVE WORST FEARS

1. Slow, gradual blood loss after rural hit-and-run car crash
2. Morbid throat swelling caused by my adult-onset avocado allergy
3. Deviated septum collapse during heavy sleep
4. Discovery of secret nickname given to me by others (e.g. Drunky, The Snotpocket, Ol' Iron Breath)
5. Rats

I realized that if a substantial amount of people were too embarrassed or scared to do what I was doing, that was a good enough reason to keep doing it.

So a bunch of us bar "poets" were invited to read at the festival the year that Nick Cave, George Clinton, the Breeders, and the Beastie Boys were on the tour. The fact that we'd be relegated to a third-stage tent managed by a temperamental drag queen named Torment and that I would be paid in daily boxed lunches didn't deter me. I decided to go. Life with the artist boyfriend was definitely on the rocks, and it occurred to me that this might be a good time to give a girl a whirl, really reach for the rainbow. And boy, in those heady days of 1994, Seattle was teeming with saucy, punk vixens. I crashed over at some other poets' apartment, some pals of the 7-Year Bitch girls we'd been hanging out with earlier, who seemed so glamorous in that dirty thermal underwear and scabies-infested sofa kind of way.

A lanky, red-haired girl and I were the last people awake at the party, and she just so happened to be moving to Paris the next day. It was a done deal. We got into bed and instead of playing it nice and naive, I decided I should take charge of the situation. I basically appointed myself the top, even though I'd never been naked in bed with a girl before. Overall, it was okay, although I didn't have an orgasm, and I do wish I had gotten her name. There's no doubt I enjoyed myself, but it was similar to the way I enjoyed waterskiing for the first time or eating uni. I jumped in with a positive attitude, realizing it was an activity beloved by millions, but it didn't exactly push me over the edge. I felt like I was doing research, and the results were coming back negative. There was a sexy, twenty-year-old girl writhing beneath me with her legs hooked over my shoulders, and I was not turned on. I was obviously some kind of sexual mutant.

Things became a little clearer as soon as I really started to hang out with a bunch of full-on dykes. These people appreciated the aesthetics of things I'd never known anyone to appreciate before, such as the art of the perfectly formed beer belly, the beauty of filthy hair, the decadence of a homespun knuckle tattoo. As someone who's never been a "joiner" or identified as being part of a community, I almost felt like I had found the chosen people. If you've ever hung out with San Francisco artist dykes, famous the world over for their nihilism and fashion sense, you'll know what I'm talking about. It started to come together. If I didn't want to sleep with a single one of these smart, wily babes, there could be no other answer. I had to be straight, right?

One summer shortly after this revelation, I traveled across the country with Sister Spit, a punk rock, all-girl, spoken word circus. I was one of twelve performers on the monster thirty-city tour and the only one who was pretty much straight. So it was six weeks of a lot of gay bars, a lot of gay crowds, and a lot of people assuming I was gay. The only awkward situation occurred in Tucson when my boyfriend's mother's girlfriend (got that?) somehow felt I had betrayed the lesbionic sisterhood by infiltrating the group.

"You're going out with Penny's son," she kept haranguing me. "So why are you even on this tour?"

I didn't have a good answer. "Because they're my friends, and they asked me to come?" I ventured.

It did little to satisfy this militant butch social worker with a silver crew cut. She and Penny later broke up, which really messed with the dynamics of their Women's Full Moon Canyon Hiking Group.

So the tour made it all the way to Provincetown (aka P-Town), a place where rainbow flags fiercely compete with rainbow wind socks for rippling space in the sea air. This was one of the most anticipated stops on the tour because:

1. We had two shows lined up. Therefore, we were able to stay in one town for two whole, consecutive days.
2. We were houseguests of all the cool dykes in town—academics and porn stars alike.
3. Everyone would certainly see some action.

The anticipation was so high that girls who had coupled up on the tour had a deal that they could split up for the two days in Provincetown and resume their affair once we left the town limits. There was also a point system in place. Someone had made a poster that hung inside the van charting everyone's sexual escapades. One star for kissing, two stars for feeling up, etc. It was the kind of thing you would expect of adolescent boys, except we were women in our mid-twenties.

When our 1978 Dodge van hit P-Town, an air siren must have been activated because we showed up at a bar crawling with locals ready to scope out the talent. It was like someone had been making the rounds on horseback announcing, "Fresh meat coming in off the Cape, sailors!" We literally made our entrance to a round of applause. These gals were fired up. I went to order a beer, and somebody had already bought it for me. As the intense pickup rituals began, I spied a good looking dude in a cowboy hat who turned out to actually be a lady named Trouble. (The modern lesbians are also aces at renaming themselves. I know Tiger, Rocket, Buzz, Silas, Sugar, Tuffy, and Steak.) Trouble and I had been chatting for approximately five minutes or so when I found out she held two jobs which complimented each other nicely—a construction worker and a retail salesclerk at the local sex toy shop. Her personal bumper sticker, for those in the habit of boiling everyone down to a single catchphrase, would most definitely include the expression "tools for the job." A few hours later, as the crowd dwindled, she asked me if I'd like to spend the night at her place.

This was a dilemma. I thought I had settled the bisexuality issue months ago, but I definitely liked this Trouble character. It was time to ask myself the hard questions: *Are you only going home with her because you haven't had sex in three weeks? Is it because you know if you hook up with her, there'll be a comfortable bed tonight and a shower in the morning instead of crashing in a sleeping bag under someone's dining room table? If you do it with her and you're not turned on, will you finally admit that you are a full-fledged heterosexual woman who happens to enjoy the company of many lesbians?*

I drained my beer, let Trouble carry my bag, and walked with her through the moonlit streets as waves crashed on the shore and people in underwear danced on the balconies around us. *I am in Provincetown in the summer,* I told myself. *I am on the arm of a hot, local stud. I am on tour. If this is not a litmus test for my bisexuality, I don't know what is. We will solve the riddle by sunrise tomorrow!*

We walked into her cottage, and I was immediately impressed by the way she had installed dimmer switches on all of her light fixtures (the benefits of dating a construction worker). She lit two square candles on the nightstand, then reached under her bed, and pulled out a toolbox.

"Why don't you choose something," she said, opening the lid to reveal an arsenal of silicone and acrylic products acquired with the employee discount that she got at her other job—the one where the terms "screw" and "hammer" were also part of the everyday lingo, but where she didn't need to wear overalls.

I perused the display, finally settling on something that wasn't too "beer can" or too "breadstick," and handed it to her.

Trouble was on it. The way she went around gathering all her gear, arranging and rearranging her love props, detailing the room for the impending *denouement*, all while whistling a jaunty little tune, made me think of the oral surgeon who had sliced open my hard palate as a teenager. The latex gloves probably contributed to that memory as well.

After a month on the road, the full day's drive, the beer, not to mention the psychological exercise of scrutinizing the politics of desire, I started to drift off.

"You still into this?" she asked, winking one of her big brown eyes at me and tugging on my big toe.

I sat up on the bed and looked out the window at the dark summer sky. I'd known the answer for a long time, but tonight I decided to finally know it once and for all.

6
ALTERNATIVE CYBER-COLUMN

Remember that brief period of time, when saying that you worked for a website sounded all sexy and cutting edge? My Internet job started just before that. It was back in the day when a lot of people threw around the term "cyberspace," and it was still ruled by a bunch of idealistic visionaries and wonky techies geeking out about the Great Equalizer without the benefit of big budgets or glamorous magazine profiles. Kind of like it was before blogs.

The company I worked for—hired by the daily paper and its affiliated television station in San Francisco to run its website—was a motley assortment of people to whom the former big rig-driving, hippie boss happened to take a shine. For example, after hearing me read a poem on the radio, he appeared at one of my readings and hired me to do statistics. Our office manager had come into his life

twenty years before. As the chief midwife on their Tennessee com-
mune, she had delivered his children.

Although the old school family who owned the paper and the
new guard idealist whom they hired to run their website didn't
have a lot in common, there was one thing they seemed to agree
on: Tom Petty sure did rock. Petty was currently doing a twenty-
night run at the Fillmore Auditorium, and during that time we
were subject to an endless array of photos of Petty rocking out the
previous night, along with shaded sidebars recapping the apparent
history-making set lists. The paper and its cadre of dinosaur music
scribes offended me on a deep level that probably had less to do
with the man or his music than with the fact that I was collating
Excel spreadsheets in a windowless basement office with a faulty
ventilation system that constantly sucked in carbon monoxide
fumes from the street above us.

Luckily, I enjoyed complaining. A news editor who was tired of
listening to me sarcastically crowing out set list highlights from the
water cooler made a suggestion—that I write my own column. "It
won't run in the newspaper or anything, but we can put it up on the
site next to the other articles," he offered. "You and your weird stuff.
You can have your own nightlife column. An alternative cyber-
column!"

In San Francisco in 1997, I was excited at the prospect of having a cyber-anything. I was still getting the lingo all wrong, talking
about logging onto the E-mail Net to Browse the Interweb, but I

knew exactly the kind of column the editor meant. I just wasn't sure that I wanted to do it. If you live near any metropolitan area, chances are there are more than a few writers devoted to covering "the nightlife beat"—the phrase itself bringing to mind a montage scene of neon-lit martini signs boozily floating past as yellow cab doors open and close with possibility. . . . A woman in a fur-collared coat glances over her shoulder, waving to friends as she is led out the door by a faceless suit firmly holding her elbow. . . . A black man raises the bell of his saxophone, takes a deep breath, and blows a startling, dangerous riff. And they're on to the next hotspot. Jazz! The Nightlife!

And alternative nightlife? The popular weekly papers in the city, often referred to as "alternative" papers, already covered most of the places I ended up at anyway. A show with three bands, a drag king, a cricket-eating dominatrix, and a guy doing BMX bike tricks out in front of an old French fry factory in a crappy neighborhood sounds alternative, but the minute it gets a snappy write-up as a "pick of the week" in a paper with a circulation of 200,000, it doesn't seem so underground anymore. The urban media is so addicted to ferreting out these "underground favorites," "hidden treasures," and "best kept secrets" that it's difficult to walk into virtually any establishment and not see a framed review or "Best of" award from some newspaper, magazine, or website that may have only existed for seven months before its venture capital ran out.

But an alternative to Tom Petty and the rest of the arena rock that the paper was covering? I could get behind that, and I kind of liked the idea of infiltrating the stodgy daily. My column would be featured right alongside the balding guy whose cat—get this—acted *so* human sometimes and the modern day Erma Bombeck whose five kids were the most quotable pack of hyenas to ever roam Noe Valley.

I approached the office conference table and peered into the three-foot-tall tin of popcorn. In any office I've ever worked, the tri-section with the caramel corn goes first, followed by that with the cheddar. I popped a few kernels in my mouth, transfixed by the Dilbert cartoon on the side of the tin. *I have a Dilbert job*, I thought, laboring over what color thumbtacks I should use to attach the day's spreadsheets to the corkboard. I should definitely try to write that column. *I might as well get paid for going out*, I told myself, until I realized that I wouldn't be getting paid right away.

First, I had to come up with a name, which is always the easiest way to spot a nightlife column. Catchy, cute, and punnier than a Carrot Top concert, nightlife columns across the country are often called things like "The Buzz," "The Fix," "The Mix," "The Word," "Nightcrawler," "Nightwatch," "Night Ranger," "The Lone Ranger," "The Socialist," "The Aesthete," "The Dilettante," "Scene and Herd," "Scene and Seen," "Kick and Scream," "Around Hear," "Hear This," "Hear and Now," "Be Hear Now," "Hear, Here," "Riff Raff," "Radar Station," "Open City," "City Lights," "City Dweller," "Nitty Gritty City," "Fan Club," "Club Sandwich," and "Club Scout." And their logos usually involved the aforementioned, and still remarkably reliable, martini glass, musical notes, crescent moon, or drawing of a young woman wearing chunky boots.

I can't remember why I thought a pseudonym was a good idea (something vague about anonymity), but I quickly discovered if you are nobody, and you are writing as a different nobody and on top of that you are writing for the Internet, it is really, really hard to get into shows free. This was my attempt to get on a guest list for the first time:

Uh, hi. I write a column for the daily paper's website? No, not the paper itself, just for the Internet. Yeah, they have this stuff up there that you can get on the computer if you have a computer with a modem. No, it's different from the paper. I mean, it's owned by them. That's who I get my paycheck from, but we have a separate office. Well, the column's about music and stuff, and I wrote a preview about tonight's show. You can look at it if you log on to the Web, the World Wide Web, and I can give you the URL to check it out. The address to find it to type into your browser. Window. It's H-T-T-P Colon Backslash. . . . Oh, okay. Anyway, I said good things and told people to go. Do you think I could get on the list? Hey, that's great! My name? It's, um, Mae. Mae Hemm.

Of course, the first time I went to the box office and Mae Hemm didn't have any ID or press pass, I was forced to pay the cover charge.

Although my days among the nubby, fabric-covered baffles of

my cubicle were brightened immeasurably by the one day a week I wrote my column, the manically snappy tone of preview journalism did start to grow a little tedious after the first, oh, sixty or seventy weeks. I'm talking about the peppy salesmanship in writing like this:

It's that time of year again for the Folsom Street Fair. When else do you get to watch leathermen in ball gags getting flogged out in the street while dildo-wielding dyke bands take off their shirts and snap-happy tourists quickly fill up the megs on their digital cameras? So grab your chaps (or somebody else's!) and head out this Saturday. Only in San Francisco! Folsom Street Fair, October 1. Noon–8:00 P.M.

The cycle was endless: performance art, poetry readings, sketch comedy, dance troupes, restaurant openings, magazine release parties, fashion shows, film festivals, strip clubs, drag bars, urban circuses, and fighting robot wars, all with varying degrees of fire and nudity. I constantly felt like I was slapping together absurdist haikus from a magnetic poetry kit with the enthusiasm and discernment of a high school cheerleader.

Come and get your flame—
eating polyamorous
trapeze artists, folks!

You know you want to
see scavenged home movies set
to theremin, right?!

Hot electroclash
interpreted by butoh
dancers in the buff!

Eventually switching to my real name helped things, if only because I was forced to take full responsibility for my own prose, but I also left the previews behind and switched to doing a weekly *wrap-up* which, although riddled with its own inherent annoyances, looked more like this:

After the man carefully parallel parked his Ford Fiesta, he pulled a leather hood out from his Guatemalan fanny pack and yanked it onto his head. He paused for a moment, went to his trunk and pulled out a bottle of water. Difficult to drink with the bondage mask. He then began patting his body, including his bare ass cheeks, in a series of gestures that made it seem like he was looking for a place to put his keys. Finally settling on removing just the car key from the ring, he inserted it down the long shaft of his knee-high boots and tossed the rest of the set onto the floorboards. With that, he headed off toward the Folsom Street Fair, followed closely by one of the performers that day, Ouchy the Adult Clown.

I think it's safe to say that the barometer of a tried-and-true urban "alternative" classic like the leather street fair scene remains fairly stable, so the idea was that I could (a) keep the column interesting by writing about what actually happened afterward as opposed to what was probably going to happen beforehand and (b) only show up for as long as it took to see something interesting. For the most part, I still enjoy these little excursions, but it helps to know that sometimes you can just slow the car down a little and rubberneck.

But then the problems began. When I was writing the previews, I could recommend up to five shows a week because I didn't have to actually go to all of them, but doing reviews meant I had to spend five nights a week going out—which, just like smoking cigarettes and wearing miniskirts, is a sign of larger issues once you're over thirty. I did it for years, but in addition to my own performance and rehearsal schedule, it got so unwieldy that pretty soon I was trying to cram as many events into one night as was humanly possible. If I timed it right, usually on a Thursday (which is still the new Friday, even though there was a bold campaign to make Monday the new Thursday a few years ago), I could start off at a cocktail reception for a new restaurant or a gallery opening, then stop by a literary reading or magazine release party, and then try to wind up at a club where hopefully the band I wanted to see was halfway done with their set already. In fact, I secretly hoped that along the way someone would fall off the stage or start break dancing badly, so I wouldn't have to try to describe guitar tone or use the word "skronky" to explain a horn sound again.

I didn't want to come off like an ungrateful ass clown (I knew I had a good gig), but I couldn't help thinking that the right person could really run with the ball, an aspiring critic or big *Sex & the City* fan who could get into playing up the generic fabulousness that goes along with free drinks and having her name on the guest list. Instead, it was me, constantly convinced I must be missing out on the real action because nearly everything I covered was also being written up in the city's other "alternative nightlife" columns by a stable of smart vixens with names like Silke, Summer, Sia, and Neva. Minor victories were tallied when one of us saw Michael Stipe dancing by himself at a dive bar as "Sister Goldenhair" looped on the jukebox, and defeats came in the form of being the last person in town to catch the PornOrchestra, an ensemble composing alternative scores to projected porn flicks.

What happened next was all my fault. In an effort to extract myself a little bit more from the whirling hamster ball of doom that is keeping up with *What's Hot!*, I suggested to my editor that I start adding in a few items of local gossip. People could e-mail tips to me while I sat at home in my underwear, spilled coffee on my keyboard, and tweezed my chin hairs. Gossip columns abounded for the socialites and celebrity set, but what about our own musicians, artists, and writers? "Excellent idea," the editor said. "Alternative gossip!"

Maybe I could even add in some of those spicy blind items they run on Page Six.

At first it seemed to be going smoothly. I went out two or three nights a week and filled in the rest of the column with harmless, upbeat gossip: a behind-the-scenes look from a filmmaker's first trip to Sundance, a local singer/songwriter handpicked by a Grammy award–winning artist to open up her national tour, a baby born to a musical fire-eating couple is named after a Frank Zappa song. But then the e-mails started. Which well-known author was seen last weekend making out with someone other than his fiancé? Which trust-fundy deejay acts all ghetto but recently bought a million-dollar house? Which raging, egotist rock star was openly doing coke at the tranny bar? And what about the stuff I knew was true like the friend at the boutique who caught a famous actress shoplifting? Or seemingly innocent things about the movie star and her newspaper editor husband, now divorced, both of whom were off-limits because I worked for his paper's website? But none of it really mattered because I didn't dare write about any of them.

I couldn't even handle the heat when I published a blind item about how a certain local band had been so aggressive trying to get booked on good bills that most of the city's club bookers were— ready for this?—*annoyed* with them. The hurt e-mails and phone calls from the band and their friends (because the scene is so small everybody knew who I was talking about) didn't let up for days. Remember, their name was not mentioned and their only crime was that they were "annoying." I got so gun-shy that if I truly didn't like certain people, and this meant if they were exceedingly self-obsessed or slept with my roommate's girlfriend or stole my friend's dead mother's engagement ring and pawned it to buy speed (which was, in fact, a crime once perpetrated by a struggling MC who was bussing tables at one of the most chichi bars in town and sleeping underneath parked cars at night), I would insert some kind of code into the item just to reassure myself that I wasn't all Suzy Cream Cheese about everything. Perhaps it would read:

> Stormy, the one-named wonder with a development deal in the works, dropped in to play a set at the X Bar last Tuesday. "I'm letting my manager call the shots," she said, scanning the room with an unlit cigarette in her hand.

That was about all the snark I could muster. That was how you knew that she owed my boyfriend two hundred bucks.

Every time I tried to slip in something innocent about Chelsea Clinton eating dinner at a restaurant or Robin Williams (widely known as the only celebrity in San Francisco, I finally put a moratorium on him) doing a surprise set of new material at a small comedy club, I'd get some smarmy voice mail from a stringer for the *National Enquirer* or *The Sun.* They'd allude to the money I could make in exchange for info. (Okay, maybe not about Robin's comedy act, but who was that lady he was with?) Even though I only had $173 in the bank and a history of doing embarrassing things for small change, I never called them back. It was demoralizing enough to have a close friend, breaking down about her marriage over dinner, stop between sobbing fits to interject, "Not for publication, okay?" An old roommate who was in a popular band once greeted me over a cereal box in the morning with the phrase, "This is off the record, but. . . ."

As the weeks went on, I began to fantasize about masterminding a random "item" generator that I could license to writers confronting similar problems. They would be able to just plug in the names like a Mad-Lib. This way, fledgling artists could get some press, but no one would be responsible for the outcome:

> **Cute girl bass player,** currently playing in a side project with the **drummer from Glitchcore Band,** was spotted at the **Dive Bar** where **Visiting celebrity** was just spied after his two-hour dinner at **Trendy Restaurant that serves macaroni and cheese and 40 ounces** wearing **latest co-opted fashion accessory.** Sources tell this columnist that after last year's fiasco involving **comic book artist** and **zine publisher's** attempt at staging a benefit show for **local filmmaker's medical procedure** in which **number** dollars was raised, no one wants to go to **Clear Channel music venue** anymore even though **popular club band** has a show there this Thursday, which is supposedly the new **day of week.** Not to

worry. Word on the street is that **record label that Kim Gordon likes** is still interested in putting out their upcoming record, apparently titled "**nasty verb**-ing the **dessert.**"

I guess I could just start rehashing some of the press releases flooding my inbox, but most of them sound like this (actual press release):

Good afternoon Beth—
Country music star Wynonna Judd adopted an arthritic dog today in New York, and I thought you might like more information about the event. Wynonna is already mom to 13 dogs, and "Pixie" makes 14. I've copied some information below, and uploaded several photos of Wynonna, Pixie and her growing "family."

After seven years of writing my column, I am nearly out of original ways to cover the "alternative" events that supposedly no one is covering even though everyone is. But on a recent Friday night, I was shocked to find myself doing the most alternative thing I could think of. With a freshly Xeroxed program in hand, I sat in row seventeen of an elementary school auditorium watching a community theater production of Andrew Lloyd Webber's *Joseph and the Amazing Technicolor Dreamcoat*. It had seventy-four cast members, including a chorus of twenty schoolchildren, and the AYSO soccer "Everybody Plays" credo extended to the dentist doing a two-step and the loan processor on piano. The enthusiasm with which the two affable moms greeted me at the door assured me that I was the only one giving this show coverage. Every other columnist was probably out covering the *Poke n' Grope*, the *Pool Toss*, or *Battlebots*, but on this night I got to be Guffman—actually showing.

What I expected to be a deliriously kitschy experience, a no-brainer that might have me ducking out at intermission to find a nearby bar, ended up being oddly compelling. I found myself amazed at how much work everyone had put in and moved by the fact that they weren't motivated by the prospect of a review or the bragging rights they'd score from playing at some cool venue. Something else was probably wrong with me at the time because the musical itself is pretty terrible, but when it got to the part in the show where everyone got to take a little solo, I started to tear up. I heard a man behind me, one of about a hundred people there with a flash camera and opening night congratulatory flowers on his lap, whisper just before his friend took a two-line "solo" in a song, "Go, Harry!"

At intermission I wandered the halls of the school, pausing at the cheesy head shots of some of the more pro thespians thumb-tacked to a corkboard and listened to a gaggle of teenage girls chat-ter about how foxy Joseph was. They wondered if he was doing it with Djuna, the narrator, whose bio revealed that she was a finalist on *American Idol*, presumably oblivious to the fact that Joseph was as gay as an Easter bonnet. Then the lights flashed, and I let out an excited yelp when I saw a cardigan-clad teacher madly flicking the switch up and down, just like all the elementary schoolteachers I ever had. I grabbed a homemade brownie from the concession stand and found my way back. The extended family and friends of the enormous cast were already in their seats, actually on the edge of them, anticipating the second half of the show. As the lights went down, I put away my pen and listened to the rustling of bouquets.

⑦ THE ONE

My boyfriend John's band, Ebola Soup, had a gig at The Stork Club in Oakland. It was the late 1990s and The Stork Club was already a tiny Bay Area legend, but you could say that Ebola Soup was still actively searching for its fan base. I was sure the experimental trombone, sludgy vocals, and refusal to play in 4/4 time had something to do with that, but all of us were hoping a few more people would come around when they released their self-produced limited edition 7" vinyl record, *Feeling Logy*.

There were only about six people in the bar so far. Micki, the owner, was chain-smoking her long, brown Mores and looking exhausted. She usually opened the place up at 7:00 A.M. for the swing shift workers and kept two cigarettes going in separate ashtrays at each end of the bar, her own little tag team of smokes, until closing. She owned the place with her husband Wes, a Vietnam vet of the clean-cut variety and one of those guys who looked like he might enjoy a little bloodshed every so often just to take the edge off.

They'd decorated the place in a Christmas-Year-Round theme, that kind of sad and trashy festive look where the animatronic figurines were slowly going bald and blanketed in a thin layer of dust, covered with cobwebs. Multicolored garlands died slow deaths all over the place, shedding their tinsel onto the mangy reindeer and into your beer. And now that it was actually December, the whole bar was in overdrive. Micki would dig out the prize items from the storeroom throughout the night. "I love Christmas," she'd sigh, blowing up another inflatable candy cane or shoving batteries into a farting elf.

There were two separate rock scenes in the East Bay at the time, kind of like the Jets and the Sharks, except they stayed far away from each other's turf, and no one could dance very well. One faction was the Gilman Street scene, the grubby punk collective made world famous once Green Day exploded, and the other was the tribe of oddballs from The Stork.

Our friend had started booking the bands at the bar, which was key because it wasn't easy for acts like Ebola Soup, Idiot Flesh, Slombis, and Fibulator to get gigs at "regular" clubs. Unlike today, no one wanted to hear Captain Beefheart–inspired rock from music theorists back then, except other music theorists who were in rock bands inspired by Captain Beefheart. These are the bands who not only silk-screened their own record covers and T-shirts by hand, but also pounded CD cases out of sheet metal, sold bars of lard at their merch tables, and raffled off flasks of homemade grain alcohol. Time signatures could go from 7/4 to 13/8, and there were usually horns, accordions, *melodicas*, or percussion instruments made from mufflers and saw blades. You could easily walk into a bar and see trapeze artists, shadow puppet theater, or an entire band playing their instruments atop giant, moss-covered tree stumps.

Micki and Wes also had a daughter, Veronica, who was retarded, developmentally disabled, learning delayed, or handicapable, depending on whom you asked during this time of acute political correctness. No one could ever decide what to say. At one point, the city of Berkeley had officially decided to use the phrase "people who use chairs as their primary means of transportation" instead of, say, "wheelchair user." You would call the movie theater for showtimes, and the message would actually say, "Theater Three is accessible to those people who use chairs as their primary means of transportation."

Veronica, who was reportedly in her late twenties, would often sit at the bar and get hit on by drunks, and when she'd had enough, her dad would hoist her up over his shoulder and carry her upstairs to a little apartment above the bar. The fact that this scene usually took place to the confusing Middle Earth-metal-math rock or Balkan punk cabaret of whatever band was playing, while someone wearing a felt vest ran around blacking everyone's teeth out with wax, made it all the more eerie. But even some of the regulars got into the scene, and it wasn't unusual to see a fifty-year-old carpet installer sporting a Giant Ant Farm T-shirt or a lady with a beehive chanting along with the lyrics to the song "Teen Devil Worshipper Jonathan Cantero's List of Activities for the 12th of October."

The first band was set up and about to start playing, even though there were fewer than ten people in the audience, including the members of the other bands, Micki, and me. They were wearing Boy Scout uniforms, and the bass drum had the band's name printed on it, Optimist International. In the middle was their logo, a hand holding up a glass that was half full.

Supposedly their drummer was the son of one of the authors of the *Chicken Soup for the Soul* series, so that explained a lot. I took one look at him and could immediately see that a childhood filled with relentless life coaching and speeches on self-empowerment had taken its toll. At about twenty-four years old, the guy looked forty. His hair was jet black and greasy, and he sported the heavy blue-black stubble of a cartoon hobo. His shoulders bore the unmistakable slope of someone constantly trying to cave in on himself and disappear. He could have made a bundle as a male model during the whole heroin chic thing. So he was the group's lady magnet, the one most girls wanted to cuddle or abuse. But it was another member of the band I couldn't take my eyes off. The singer/guitarist was clearly a superstar, according to my standards for men, which I was just beginning to realize were rather unorthodox.

Looking like a skinny, young David Letterman with bulging blue eyes and an extremely expressive set of pillow lips, he shouted into the mic, "This song is called the Wack-ass Caucasian Two-step

Chicken, and I think you're really going to like it a lot!" At that point, he smiled wide and then seemed to completely lose control of his faculties. He dropped down to the floor on his back. There he lay, spasming and freaking out for a second before popping back up on his feet and continuing: "She told me to do The Wack!" The way he played his guitar sounded like he was constantly tuning and retuning it.

"She told me to do the Wack-ass!"

His singing style was a frantic yelp.

"She told me to do the Wack-ass Caucasian Two-step Chicken!"

My boyfriend at the time, Ebola John, was seated on a black banquette against the wall restringing his guitar. He was yet another one of these unconventional studs, if I may take liberties with how most of society defines that word. He had a large beak-like nose, a solid little beer gut, and spindly arms and legs. The secret to his hair was to wash it with Ivory soap at night and sleep on it—no combs or brushes, no styling product to help it look messy, just a pillow and a good ten hours of sleep. With no effort whatsoever, he had the kind of look celebrities pay stylists to achieve for them and was completely clueless that he even had it. The best part of all, however, was that after graduating magna cum laude from UC—Berkeley with a degree in biochemistry, he was offered full-ride scholarships to graduate school at Harvard and M.I.T., both of which he turned down to play the guitar. Awesome.

I looked back up at the stage and saw the David Letterman guy crouched in some kind of yoga squat, trying to duckwalk across the front of the stage. He jumped down into the audience, ran to the bar, and hoisted himself up on top of it, presenting everyone with a gift-wrapped and autographed copy of *Chicken Soup for the Soul: A Third Helping*. His brand of dorkiness was like nothing I'd ever seen before, combining an admirable lack of self-consciousness with the showmanship of an enthusiastic, although substandard, theater student. And then later, when I found out he was nearly legally blind without the thick horn-rimmed glasses that had belonged to his Grandfather Gus, that was it. I was smitten.

A year of Sundays spent listening to four-hour Stockhausen operas with Ebola John passed. While living with him, I had learned to correctly pronounce the names of Polish composers, fall asleep listening to minimalist Morton Feldman records, and prepare a Sicilian dish using a thistle called a cardoon. As much as I loved him and his ability to put on solo concerts using only his guitar, a fork, and a vibrator, we both knew it was time to hang it up. Luckily, dating low-key, introverted artists had always made for drama-free breakups. You decided who took the records and who took the books and then went to have a beer and split the tab. (Incidentally, Ebola Soup also broke up and some other band called Ebola Joe and The Children McNuggets started doing gigs around town. The members of Ebola Soup made the distinction that, unlike their own band, Ebola Joe et al. had obviously formed *after* the publication of the bestseller about the Ebola virus, *The Hot Zone*, which, duh, said a lot about how orig-inal their music must have been. They probably even played in 4/4.)

About a week after I moved out, I went alone one night to see Optimist International play at a dive in San Francisco—one of those places where the stage is just a section of the floor in the cor-ner that's been taped off. Someone in the audience had brought photos from the band's Valentine's Day show, and if the spectacle in front of me wasn't enough to refuel my crush, the pictures of Eli wearing nothing but a pair of cherub wings and an adult diaper sealed the deal. He looked like a nerdy, angry angel.

One of the magic ingredients in most of my romances, be they short-or long-term, had always been alcohol. This night was no dif-ferent. After they finished playing, I bought Eli a beer, and he apol-ogized for being so sweaty, which I found impressive (not that he apologized, but that he sweated so much).

"What was that one song?" I asked him. "All the feedback, I couldn't really . . . something about 'God's Day' or something?"

"Oh, yeah," he said, wiping the sweat from his face with a ran-dom tube sock produced from I don't know where because he was still wearing two striped ones that went up to his knees. "It's about how the meter maids let people park in the median on Sunday be-cause they're going to church, but if you park in the median and you're not going to church, they give you a ticket."

"That is so true," I said. "It's like, if you're Christian, you can break the law, but if you're not, you get fined by the city!"

What else was there to say, really? We had made the connection necessary to lead us, three minutes later, to go outside and make out on the hood of my truck.

I happened to be in the middle of what was a long period of sporadic and marginal housing situations. At the time, I was subletting a room in my friend's one bedroom apartment. This meant that technically I was sleeping in her living room, except that the living room had been turned into a bedroom by the person I was subletting from. I had to pay only $125 a month, but there was one catch: Every Tuesday night I had to sleep somewhere else. The girl I subletted from had almost moved into her boyfriend's house, but Tuesday was their designated night to have their own "space," or however that works when couples go to therapy or read books on boundaries. Tonight happened to be a Tuesday.

Usually I set up a place to sleep ahead of time, rotating through various flats and apartments around the neighborhood. Sometimes I house-sat for coworkers or crashed on the couches of acquaintances. Occasionally, I stayed in the extra bedroom of the guitarist for a legendary San Francisco band who would wake me up for work in the morning by playing dirges on an old reed organ. I'd walk out my door and see him down the hall, seated on the bench in a silk bathrobe, his bald head keeping time. Without looking at me, he'd lift a hand off the keys and point to the kitchen, where he'd laid out a proper coffee service on the table. But this night, I had no plan.

"Feel free to sleep in my bed with me if you can't find something," my roommate said on my way out. Then she thought twice: "Well, maybe put your ear to the door first and see if it sounds like anybody else beat you to the punch."

After a half hour or so of frantic kissing to the sound track of rumbling buses and drunken heckling, I remembered that I had to be at work at 8:30 the next morning. So I did what I thought most responsible people in my situation would do: I said good-bye to Eli, went back to the apartment, took a shower, and put on the clothes I would wear to work the next day. Then I walked over to his warehouse at 3:30 A.M. with my toothbrush.

I banged my keys against the glass like he told me to, trying to not be too loud because I didn't want to disturb the two homeless guys passed out in the doorway. And then Eli opened the door, wearing only a smile. Okay, I'm just kidding, but that was his original plan.

"I thought it would be funny to answer the door naked and be like, 'What? You don't think I'm sexy? Standing here in this dirty warehouse, naked in the dark?' Or maybe I'd just be wearing a powdered wig. But then I freaked out when you knocked and put my clothes back on."

He took my hand and led me through the front room of the 5,000 square foot space, a fire-damaged, former sewing sweatshop that he and his friends had talked the landlord into illegally renting to them for cheap. It seemed especially auspicious because it was during the dot-com boom, and they could have rented out the space for about $15,000 a month instead of $1,500.

"We occasionally have some problems," he said as I stepped over a dismantled motorcycle and rammed my shin against a statue of Vladimir Lenin. "Like the junkies in the hotel upstairs leave their sinks running, and there's some leakage or, um, some other stuff goes wrong sometimes." His voice was trailing off. "But they like renting to us because they never have to fix anything."

They also let Eli and his roommate, the Chicken Soup guy, run a weekly music series out of the place. Some of the best improv jazz and rock musicians in the country played there, in this dingy, old warehouse, every Saturday night. Nearly everyone who'd ever played with John Zorn had a show there, including Otomo Yoshihide, the Japanese noise star, and when saxophonist Steve Lacy came to San Francisco from Paris a few years before he died, his only local show was at Eli's house.

We went back to his bedroom, a windowless cell that he had drywalled and in which he had built a sleeping loft. It smelled kind of like wood glue and the rosin for his upright bass, and there were a bunch of framed pictures around that I took a second to check out. One was of a woman who was obviously his mother, as she looked *exactly* like him—shaved head, big glasses, standing in front of Good Vibrations, the local sex toy store. I kept myself from blurting out, "Wow, so you're mom's a lesbian."

Insert sex scene here.

Approximately three hours later, I was startled out of my sex haze by some guy yelling in Arabic. It sounded like he was in the same room. He was shouting over a radio blasting staticky soft jazz.

"Who the fuck is that?" I asked. It sounded like it was coming from inside his room.

Eli, sweeping his hand around the perimeter of the bed for his glasses, didn't seem fazed at all. "It must be seven already," he said. "The liquor store's opening up."

It turns out his cave did have a window. It opened up into the neighboring liquor store.

The guy kept yelling, and soon somebody else was yelling back at him. I heard the radio station's catchphrase: "Soft and warm, the quiet storm."

That's when Eli bolted up, threw his shoe against the wall, and shouted something I didn't understand.

I had heard from a friend that night at the bar that he spoke German, Spanish, and Russian, but enough was enough.

"You speak *Arabic?*" I asked, searching for my underwear in the blankets.

"No, not really," he said quickly. I was sure he was lying in that way people do when they're all embarrassed about being a genius. "I only know a couple phrases."

But I had seen the way his mouth moved. All the language geniuses I had ever met looked perfectly normal when they were speaking their native language, but as soon as they busted into another one, it changed. Suddenly their teeth appeared to be too large for their mouths, their lips got all pouty, or their tongue went into overdrive. The language had possessed them. One minute they were in front of me ordering a cappuccino from the counter person at a café, and then they turned around and bumped into their Norwegian friend, and suddenly it was like a horror movie—like a different person was trapped inside them. I got up to go to the bathroom, still envisioning the way his mouth just did that thing, thinking I'd never met anyone like him. As I was climbing down the stairs of the loft, he suddenly sat up and said, "Wait!"

"What?"

He looked extremely apologetic. "Um. Just be careful of . . ." He paused.

"Be careful of what?"

Here I'd spent the whole night in his warehouse, and I obviously had no problem dodging bums, tripping over junk in the dark, climbing up to the loft, and waking up to the sound of the liquor store dudes fighting. I couldn't possibly imagine what could be found between here and the bathroom that would surprise me. Cockroaches, syringes, ex-girlfriends, surveillance equipment, I'd thought of it all. I honestly wouldn't have been surprised if one of his roommates had bought some land mines over the Internet for an art project or decided to dig a moat outside the door while we were sleeping.

"What is it?" I asked.

"When you go through the kitchen," he said, "just watch out."

I gave him a look that told him he better just come out with it.

I wasn't going to ask again. He took off his glasses and rubbed his hand over his face.

"One: I'm really glad you like me. And two. . . ."

"What's two? Tell me two."

He crawled a little bit closer.

"Just keep your eyes out for the feral raccoons."

A BED AND A BREAKFAST

"Lookin'? One and one. One and one. Outfits. Chiva, chiva. One and one. Outfits. Lookin'?"

It got so exhausting having people constantly assume I was a drug addict. I was spending a lot of time at Eli's warehouse at Sixteenth and Mission, one of the city's biggest drug intersections, and it got to the point where I could gauge how haggard I looked on a given day by how many people tried to sell me drugs on the two block walk to buy my coffee and bagel. The dark circles under my eyes had been there for years, so at least they were finally getting some props. But there were days when I'd gotten a good night's sleep and bothered to put on lipstick, and I'd still be hounded by offers the second I stepped out the door.

One morning—it must have been close to the end of the month when everybody's public assistance checks were running out, when the neighborhood got really gnarly—a scab-covered but otherwise adorable street urchin approached me. She couldn't have been more than fifteen.

"One and one? Outfits? Chiva? One and one?"

For those of you not familiar with the parlance of San Francisco street drugs in the late 1990s, one and one is a bag of heroin and a bag of cocaine for doing speedballs. An outfit is a syringe. Chiva is heroin.

"Oh, no thanks," I said, as if she were offering me a glass of orange juice after I'd just brushed my teeth.

"One and one, one and one?" she continued, apparently not convinced.

I was at the curb waiting for the light to change, staring straight ahead now.

"Chiva? You want some chiva?"

She was obviously a runner, a kid sent out by the main dealers to drum up business. Every referral she gave the dealer earned her credit toward free goods and services for herself. Like something your chiropractor or dry cleaner does. She tugged on my sleeve. "One and one! One and one!"

Jesus, she should really be a Girl Scout with this kind of hard sell. All this crap on the news about how unhealthy Thin Mints were and how the kids were being "pimped" by the Girl Scout Association of America to "push" trans fat had me visualizing that all the drug runners *were* Girl Scouts. Dressed up in little uniforms with ripped tights, they could earn syringe-shaped badges and go to camp under the freeway on-ramp.

I kept staring straight ahead, and when the light changed, she followed on my heels through the crosswalk, barking in her baby druggie voice, "One and one! Chiva! One and one!"

I kind of wanted to swat her (nothing too violent, just a really quick backhand like you see moms do in supermarkets) or at least file a complaint with her superior. I stopped at the opposite corner to wait for the next light, and when she didn't let up, I tilted my head down, looked right into her big, crazed eyeballs and said in a monotone, "SFPD. Keep moving."

Her face fell, and she skittered away, filling me momentarily with the soul-warming hubris of superiority.

That night I told Eli and some of his friends about my new trick, thinking of it as a valuable tip they might want to co-opt for themselves. "Oh, no," one of them said. "That's bad. That's really bad."

"What?" I asked, oblivious to why he was suddenly on doom patrol. "It worked great."

"If they think you're a narc, and they see you coming out of our house. . . . oh, man."

All of them sat around shaking their heads, amazed at my idiocy, quizzing me on what she looked like, speculating on whether she might be working for Rafael, Duke, or perhaps Bearded John. I suppose it was not unlike announcing to your Neighborhood Watch association that you were actually a burglar and would be sitting tight until they let up their guard. It made me defensive. Were we seriously discussing what, God forbid, Bearded John would think of us? In one fell swoop, I had now ruined the relationships everyone in the warehouse had with the greater community of drug addicts in the Mission District area because I lied about being a cop to an underage junkie, a junkie who could have been dead by then, back home with her parents, or so fucked up she wouldn't remember my face if I'd been Mary Kate *and* Ashley Olsen.

It was about this time that Eli and I decided we needed to go on vacation. Just get away from what could be politely referred to as the "hustle and bustle of the city," but what was more accurately nonstop verbal assaults and a vomit-covered front door. The novelty of kicking over Snapple bottles full of pee everywhere I went was finally wearing off.

Also, to drive the point home, we opened the newspaper one morning to see a photo of a guy running for mayor. In the picture, the candidate, a former police chief, was gesturing broadly to a dilapidated storefront with cardboard propped in a broken window and a bent metal gate. His facial muscles were tight, his nose a bit pinched, as if he had been holding his breath for quite a while, praying for the shutter to finally click on his photo op. The caption read, "Jordan says abandoned storefronts make the Mission District look like 'a bombed out Beirut.'" The "abandoned" graffiti-covered warehouse in the background was, of course, Eli's house.

My mom had called me at work because it was the only place she could ever find me. "Yeah, we're thinking of going on vacation,"

I told her. "You know, to get away from the, uh, the hustle and bustle of the city."

"You should go to a B and B!" she said. "That's a perfect getaway. There are a lot of cute ones in Napa!"

I knew she was just trying to be helpful, but Eli and I were about as remote from being a B and B couple as Bearded John and his teenage protégé. We just weren't Bubbling Brook Inn or Enchanted Cottage material. Somehow, Eli already knew this about himself without ever having gone to one. I had learned the hard way.

Sometime in the mid-eighties, the idea that you might want to pay to spend a weekend sharing a house with strangers in a contrived country setting somehow got shoved over the transom and fell into the ever-expanding, handwoven basket of bourgeoise leisure activities. People began flocking to restored Victorians and quaint farmhouses, reclining on floral duvets next to rustic end tables equipped with decorative pitchers sitting in basins in which you could "make your toilet" before the dinner bell rang, and you filed downstairs to dine on duck's breast and engage in awkward conversation with the proprietors—an investment banker and a marketing consultant—who had decided to get out of the rat race and fulfill their dreams of being the "just folks" ambassadors of the hospitality industry.

I resented the fact that when I finally came down to breakfast in one of these places, the hostess had seemingly been standing by the oven, warming my mini-orange-cardamom muffins for hours until, upon hearing my footsteps, she raced across the parquet to grab the quilted calico hen to put them in before they cooled off. She would pretend to be surprised by my arrival, but would actually be quietly seething that my tardiness had cut into her potpourri-making or ikebana time. I was not the kind of person she had gone into this business to meet—an unkempt nonprofessional who had nothing interesting to tell her and wasn't in the mood for her home-made apple butter that morning.

I would return from these trips emotionally exhausted from trying to avoid human contact for my entire visit, wishing for nothing more than blackout curtains, cable TV, and a centrally located ice machine. It was just not relaxing to have to worry about how loudly I had sex, what kind of stuff I left in the wastebasket, and what I wore when I went down the hall in the middle of the night to pee. Plus, my idea of vacation didn't include getting bullied into a game of Scattergories by a couple from New Hampshire celebrating their twenty-eighth wedding anniversary. (That particular couple had been nice at first, a little grabby, but the husband didn't have to corner us up against the butter churn like that.)

"Yeah. That's a really good idea, Mom," I said, trying to sound upbeat, as if I hadn't kicked a sleeping prostitute out of my car that morning. "Maybe we'll do that."

In reality, we had decided the best place to get away from it all was Tokyo. My best friend was living there, and we figured that with all the money we could save by staying at her place and cooking meals instead of eating in restaurants, it wouldn't be that much more expensive than charging the plane tickets on our credit cards.

We left San Francisco, all burned out and broke, and for two weeks we did nothing more than ride bicycles to temples, drink large beers, take advantage of the napping rooms in public bathhouses, and watch sumo. By the end of the trip, we were ready to jump back on board the crushing cycle of chaos and excitement that typically comes with being underemployed in the creative arts sector of urban existence (electricity turned off one minute, backstage passes to Patti Smith the next). Or, the car didn't start to get you to the concert on time one minute, someone had stolen your wallet and the bouncer wouldn't let you in without your ID the next.

When we arrived home at the airport, we realized that none of our friends would be awake to pick us up at this early hour, which was sometime after 10:00 A.M. My parents and their friends were always driving one another to the airport, waking up at 4:30 A.M. to get Carole and Bob to their plane on time or being chauffeured home from a trip by Mary Claire and George. I envied them, but I didn't understand exactly how it worked. Organizing a ride home ahead of time would have meant figuring out our travel schedule, somehow relaying this information to another party who happened to own a car, and then counting on them to actually remember it when the date came. It seemed beyond anyone's skill set at the time.

We wound up springing for a door-to-door shuttle service instead of taking public transportation because neither of us had slept on the twelve-hour flight, and we were exhausted. All we wanted was to eat a big American breakfast and get in bed.

"Okay!" the driver said once we were situated. "We got Hyatt, Hyatt, Civic Center Ramada, Marriott. . . ." He paused and looked at us. "Sixteenth and Mission? Just right there on the corner?"

"Pretty much," Eli said, "just right there on the corner."

When we got to Mission Street, you might have thought we were on safari, the way everybody was peering out the windows, looking relieved to be safely behind glass. My first reaction was to be defensive, stand up, hold a fake megaphone to my mouth, and say, "Those of you on the left side of the van have a fantastic view of a black man ripping out a car antenna to fashion an ad hoc pipe with which to smoke his rock cocaine, commonly known by its street name as crack." Instead I just rolled my eyes, reminding myself that it was okay. People could live entirely functional lives without passing someone with an abscessed leg who was throwing up on the street every day.

It was a pretty dingy day, cold and gray, and after being in Tokyo—with its clean streets, bright colors, and soothing, orderly hubbub—our neighborhood looked especially squalid. Finally, we pointed to a building with shopping carts parked out front, where a guy had a blanket laid out and was having a permanent sidewalk sale. His inventory included stolen electronics, bootlegged exercise videos, and a large pair of gardening clogs.

"That's it," we said. "There's our house."

"Whoa, Mom!" said this one teenage boy wearing headphones, pointing to a roaming homeless man. "That dude is like the Michelin Man."

We dragged our stuff onto the curb and unlocked the front door, laughing in that halfhearted way people do when they're trying to shake something off, when they're pretty sure people might still be looking at them, and they want to appear as if they are in on the joke. Originally, we had both been going for that brand of "You poor, poor unsuspecting tourists with your clean hotel rooms and luggage with working zippers who are all freaked out by the harsh, gritty realism of the world you choose to ignore!" But we weren't really feeling it now. We just wanted to dump our stuff off, eat an omelet, and sleep all day.

When we wrenched open the glass door, we immediately heard a strange sound. Rather it was a familiar sound insofar as it sounded like rain, but strange because it sounded like rain coming from inside the house. Then this is what we saw: Huge metal garbage cans all around the front room overflowing with dirty, brown water. They were sitting in puddles surrounded by fresh water tracks, looking like they'd been filled and emptied over and over. The warehouse smelled as if every musty ship in the Pirates of the Caribbean ride at Disneyland had been filled with every dirty diaper of every child who'd ever ridden it. We looked up and saw the exposed pipes gushing water from about six different places.

We ran back to the kitchen to find all of Eli's roommates sitting in the red vinyl booth around the Formica kitchen table, smoking cigarettes and looking extremely glum—like characters in a German movie from the 1970s. Most of them were wearing rain gear. One was holding an umbrella over her head.

"What the fuck is going on?" Eli yelled.

No one moved at first, and then someone said, "It's been going on since four this morning. The landlord's in Jerusalem."

We ran back to Eli's room, dodging falling water in the hall, and saw that it was dripping in there as well. Someone had put a couple of pots and pans out, probably hours ago, and the floor was soaked. That's when it dawned on me. This water was coming from the pipes located *above us*—the pipes of *the residential hotel* located above us, the pipes of the residential hotel located above us that *carried water from their showers and their sinks, and most regrettably, water from the flushing of their toilets.*

Here is a horrible truth: It's possible to be elitist about excrement. I wish it weren't so, but it disturbed me so very deeply that the shit and piss that were raining down on us came from the insides of the kind of people it did. Witnessing the daily antics of my neighbors, the overdoses and brawls, the hacking coughs and subsequent loogie hocking, the needle sharing and open sores, made me convinced that I was instantaneously contracting tuberculosis, hantavirus, hepatitis, impetigo, and HIV. Not that I imagine an unexpected shower of Kennedy crap or Getty pee would be any more pleasant or necessarily virus-free, but combine the term "residential hotel" with the term "human waste," and you'll probably agree that there was substantial reason to panic.

Summoning a kind of Sigourney Weaver-esque intensity, I pulled off my T-shirt, tied it over my nose and mouth, and in my bra headed toward my belongings. "I'm going in!" I yelled for my own benefit. Everything I owned was in that room. I didn't want the warehouse to win.

Eli ran out to the street and started leaning on the landlord's buzzer. "You need to go down there and look at what is happening," he screamed at the guy who answered the door, instantly reminding me that he was an ex-theater major and the son of a single, working, Jewish mom who didn't take any crap. "We are down there being rained on by a constant flow of shit!"

The landlord's brother was probably in the middle of saying, "I don't know what to do about it," when he just decided to shut the door instead.

Meanwhile, all the inhabitants of the forty-five-room hotel were going about their daily routines. Every time a shower was turned on, whiskers were rinsed down the drain, or a toilet was flushed, a surge of water would spray down from the pipes.

Although the warehouse was a commercial space being illegally rented out as a residence, one of Eli's roommates got on the phone to try to call the local tenants' rights organization and the city water department. That's when we realized it was Memorial Day, and everything was closed.

I had made it to my stuff and was trying to quickly assess what could be salvaged, so I could get it out of there as soon as possible. Would I really wear the 1970s tennis dresses with the matching granny panties? Was I ever going to get five people together for a night of playing The Ten Commandment Bible board game? How many animal-shaped cookie cutters did one person need? Every so often, a new part of a pipe would burst and something in my safe pile would get trickled on. The roommates had already covered most of their belongings with tarps and plastic bags, but I decided I had to get everything I wanted out of there permanently. Two boxes of my books were drenched, and I wasn't going near them. Another one looked okay, but when I picked it up, the bottom dropped out. A pile of vintage jackets seemed fine, but then I had to go and touch them. Damp. A crate of letters and photos was topped by small bits of, what was it? Oh my God, it was toilet paper.

I put on my shirt and ran down the street to a budget storage locker place. It wasn't one of those kinds that looked like an impenetrable military complex or was decorated with bright orange flags. It didn't even have a logo or, from what I could tell, an actual name. It was just a warehouse with a stenciled sign above it that said "Storage." I walked into an office, and two guys in their thirties were sitting there passing a joint.

"Whoa, sorry," one of them said, waving his hand in front of his face. I almost turned around to see if they were talking to a high school principal behind me. I love situations where, for some reason, although nobody involved is really expecting it, there's still a shred of propriety intact. "We don't usually do this," his friend said.

"I don't care if you guys are stoners," I said, a bit baffled. "I just need a locker." The first guy took me back through the maze of aisles, which weren't actually arranged in rows or marked in any way, and showed me a plywood closet with a number scrawled in red Sharpie on the door.

"You can bring your own lock, but I recommend you buy a special heavy duty one from us because there are a lot of people coming in and out of here and, you know, we can't take responsibility for our clientele."

Across the way, a lady was crouched inside her closet in her underwear and a tank top, eating a piece of chicken.

I signed the contract and said I'd be right back with my stuff. I noticed that against one of the walls, there was a fleet of hand trucks. Our friend had borrowed my car while we were in Japan, and I wanted to move everything right away. "Can I use one of those to haul my stuff over here?" I asked. "I'm just two blocks up the street."

"Sorry, those are really expensive, and the wheels get messed up on the sidewalk," he said flicking his cigarette lighter on and off in front of his face. "Those are only for use inside the facility."

I started to leave, wondering how many trips it was going to take me to carry all of my stuff over by hand. Maybe I could find a skateboard or throw everything onto a piece of cardboard and drag it. Most of it was ruined anyway, so it probably wouldn't make much of a difference.

"You're welcome to use one of those," he said, pointing to a far wall across from the office. "People leave them here and sort of take them in and out all day."

I turned my head slowly, and eventually my eyes landed on what he was referring to: three banged-up shopping carts. Would I like to transport my belongings down the street in one of those? Realizing it was my best option, I silently moved toward them. Then, staring vacantly into middle distance, I backed one up and headed out onto Mission Street.

With my head bowed, I rolled down the sidewalk until I heard someone say, "Hey, girl." I looked up and saw that it was Sylvester, a sweet, on-again, off-again heroin addict who had lost his girlfriend a few months before to the terrible flesh-eating bacteria that had been written up in the papers. He was pushing his own cart toward me.

"Hey," I answered softly, maneuvering around a guerrilla art installation of TV sets, computer equipment, and stuffed animals. I kind of liked the fact that he wasn't fazed at all by the sight of me pushing around a shopping cart. One day you've got a place to live; one day you don't. It happens all the time.

When I got back to the warehouse, someone from the fire department had finally showed up and shut off the water to the entire building. Mostly, it was my kitchen stuff that survived. My parents had given me the most expensive items I owned—a blender and a mixer—plus I had a pretty extensive collection of cookbooks. I had actually bought the cookbooks with my own money and was extremely averse to throwing them away. I willed myself into thinking they looked fine, although a few of the covers seemed a tad moist. I just tore all the covers off, piled the books in a crate, and set them in my shopping cart.

On my last trip to the warehouse, I ran into Eli's friend Jake. Jake was a performance artist who used to live at the space, but had recently moved into a nicer warehouse next door with another performance artist named Jennifer. I liked Jake's work, which usually involved playing elaborate pranks or games without necessarily getting the consent of the other "participants." Jake had a great sense of humor, but Jennifer's stuff just seemed like the kind of confusing exhibitionism that gave performance art its bad reputation.

For instance, I once watched her do a piece where she pretended to be a cat burglar in a body stocking prowling around with a loot sack. After a protracted, somewhat distressing striptease amidst the audience, she got down on the floor and air-humped a pile of fake gold jewelry. Then for a finale, she doused her naked body with a bottle of champagne. (On second thought, just typing that out, it sounds pretty entertaining.) Some of her other work involved photographing herself dressed up like a hooker, circa the early 1980s, and driving around town in a souped-up muscle car that she'd had customized with an $8,000 gold-flecked paint job.

Jake said they were having a going away party for Jennifer because she was headed off on one of her semiannual trips to Thailand where she would make money. None of us knew there was an audience for performance art in Thailand, but she always came back loaded.

I hadn't realized it, but while Jake was talking, I had propped my foot up on the bottom of the cart and was hunching over the handlebar, dozing. Suddenly, in my semiconscious state, it dawned on me: Maybe we could sublet Jennifer's room while she was gone.

By the time we showed up for the party, we had been awake for thirty-six straight hours and hadn't eaten a meal or taken a shower since Tokyo. Jennifer had already been alerted to our situation, and when we walked in, she ceremoniously stood up, thrust her key at us, and plopped back down on the couch, waving off our promise of a check with a big "Okay, whatever." Her boyfriend Pete, who by a weird coincidence also happened to be the grandson of the Catholic deacon at my parents' parish in the suburbs, was sitting next to her, nodding out. He'd been a drunk since he was a teenager, but lately had taken up smoking heroin, and his social skills had really gone downhill. (A week later, he would undergo an elaborate, painful operation to detach his contact lenses from his corneas because, depressed by Jennifer's absence, he had gone on a serious bender and hadn't removed them for days.)

At some point, a fight broke out when this guy Luke, who had already served jail time for assaulting someone with a hammer, came out of Jake's bedroom swinging . . . a hammer. If you've ever seen underweight men on opiates fighting or trying to break up a fight of other underweight men on opiates, you'll understand how upset I was not to have had a video camera. But as the brawl continued and I started looking around at all these messed up people I was with, I lost it. I walked out onto Mission Street and started crying until two homeless guys tried to console me by offering a sip of their Cisco, a fruity malt beverage that eventually makes you want to destroy things.

Remember how on *Laverne & Shirley*, just when the girls would be talking about something disgusting, like "What's all this gunk on the bottom of my shoe?", Lenny and Squiggy would make their entrance and say, "Hello, girls!" What happened next was like that. I was standing there against the building, sniffling, wondering how I'd suddenly wound up with all these losers in my life. What kind of turn had my life taken that I was now standing out on Mission Street in the middle of the night after having all of my belongings ruined by a shit storm while junkie thieves swung hammers around the place that I was lucky enough to move into because a performance artist was off making cash in Thailand to help possibly pay for her boyfriend's alcoholic cornea accident? How did this happen? Just as that thought was sweeping over my brain like a poisonous cloud of gas, Eli came out of the door and said, "Hello, plum!"

He put his arm around me, and we walked to an all-night diner and ate our first meal of the day, a big breakfast. We would sleep on the warehouse floor that night and starting the following day, we would stay at Jennifer's place for a month. Our first home together.

Six months later, I went to retrieve my stuff from the storage space. I opened the door to the locker and the overwhelming stench told me some of it wasn't as "clean" as I had remembered it to be. I held my breath, carried a few boxes through the maze, and dumped them into the trash. When I walked out a few minutes later with my cookbooks, a stack of letters, and some clothes, I saw a guy in a matador jacket leaning against a wall wearing a pair of my tights around his neck and paging through one of my high school yearbooks.

And now whenever I open up my Fannie Farmer cookbook to get the recipe for banana bread, I pretend not to notice a small liquid stain seeping in from the binding on the opposite page. I start measuring out the ingredients and tell myself it's just coffee.

BROKELEY

The reason I was able to buy a house in the San Francisco Bay Area during the dot-com explosion had a little something to do with my brother, Chris, throwing a rusty butcher knife at my eye twenty years earlier.

After my dad finished his MBA while simultaneously working full-time as an engineer at Lockheed, he found that he had a lot of extra time on his hands. There were now approximately eight hours left in the day when he wasn't sleeping or haggling over bombs. Why not dabble in real estate?

My dad put a down payment on a little tract house in San Jose, and soon landlording became his hobby. I can barely remember a time when he wasn't running around with eggshell-colored semi-gloss splattered in his hair and a plunger in the trunk of his car.

When Father's Day rolled around, I'd envy all the other kids who could pick out generic Hallmark cards that featured lazy dads scratching their balls while watching a football game. It amazed me that other kids could actually go to the drugstore, pluck out one of those little, knobby statues with the carnival lettering that said "Eat, Sleep, and Golf" or "Sailors Do It Between the Sheets" and be done with it. Dads like theirs seemed like exotic beasts, rare specimens who probably also took naps and went "fishing with the boys." The closest thing my dad had to "boys" was the motley assortment of alcoholics and illegal immigrants he called on when he needed an extra hand at one of his properties. For our Father's Day presents, my brothers and I had to wrap boxes of wood screws, or we'd spend all day with construction paper creating specialty coupon books: "This Coupon Redeemable for One Hour of Silent Weeding" and "Holder Entitled to Whine-Free Grout Scraping" and so on.

My household chores had formerly included spraying the coffee tables with Endust and testing the pH-balance of the swimming pool, but I was now rousted early on the weekends and shuttled off to toil away at remote locations. Year after year, my dad had slowly acquired more houses or flipped old ones. By the time I was in fourth grade, life had become a never-ending episode of *This Old House*, except set in a series of 1960s stucco bungalows with a crew of un-skilled child laborers. It's not fair to say that we were indentured servants because my dad let us know we could walk at any time, specifically onto one of the many neighboring freeway on-ramps with our thumbs extended. And we did receive pay for our work. After we piled into the wood-paneled station wagon, my dad would swing by Winchell's for a box of doughnuts. We got three apiece to tide us over until my mom showed up with McDonald's at noon.

The butcher knife incident took place one Saturday afternoon at a duplex in Campbell, during the first season of *Charlie's Angels*. I was wearing my new iron-on Jaclyn Smith T-shirt, taking the risk that it might get dirty if we had to dig up the sewer line. By early afternoon, I had already ruined my favorite cutoff shorts by accidentally sitting down in a tray of paint to pull a nail out of my foot, so I thought the worst was over.

Chris and I were working in the front yard when he found an old knife buried in the weeds. He had been an aspiring soldier since the age of four. Whenever we couldn't find him, all we had to do was go out to this pile of dirt at the side of our house. There Chris would be, staging elaborate battles with his collection of army men or torturing them with a ball of twine and a box of Strike Anywhere matches. So he picked up the knife and started hacking away, wielding it like it a machete.

"I'm cutting through the jungles of Saigon!" he yelled with a crazed look in his eye. "There's nips and gooks all over the place! I'm gonna bring home an ear!"

He swung the knife and it flew out of his hand, traveling approximately ten feet in the air, the tip of it puncturing the inner corner of my left eye. Chris took one look at the blood gushing from my nose and mouth and pouring down my face, and screamed, "I killed her! I killed my sister!" and ran off, leaving me shocked and alone on the lawn. My mom rushed out of the house and got me into the Pinto, where she reclined the front seat until I started choking on blood. We decided it was better that I just sit up and let the whole mess run down Jaclyn's pretty little face. She held my hand and promised to get me a new T-shirt the next day.

The emergency room story is one of my mom's favorites, a defining moment in her mythology of me as a "strong girl"—or, to translate in real people language, a "stoic masochist." After receiving two shots of anesthesia in the face, I was subject to a series of Plexiglas tubes being inserted down into my tear duct to make sure it hadn't been damaged. I just kind of laid there quietly staring at the ceiling, thinking about whether I would get a new Jaclyn shirt or whether I should replace it with the one of all three Angels holding guns in a cool silhouette. After seven or eight attempts at inserting tubes of varying diameters, the doctor admitted he wasn't really sure if he was doing it correctly. A few hours later, as my mom grew restless, they eventually called in the head of the ophthalmology department, who gave me another shot; sunk the proper tube in; stitched me up with thick, black thread; and released me. I swaggered out into the parking lot, still barefoot, with my paint-covered shorts and bloody T-shirt, my face smeared and crusty, and immediately went over to my friend Amy's house to show off. I scared the shit out of her usually unflappable mother, Kathy, when I rang the doorbell, looked up at her with the knife (which I had swiped off our kitchen counter as a battle trophy) angled just right, and said, "Can Amy come out and play?"

More than twenty years later, I'm sure the knife incident must have been in the back of my dad's mind when he finally sold that house in Campbell and decided to give me some of the money to help me buy a place of my own. He did it for my brothers as well, calling it our early inheritance. My dad maintained he was doing this so he could finally stop changing my address in his computer database every four months, but I think he also knew that this way, with him alive and in charge, nobody would screw things up. All that was required of me was to take out a loan for the remaining amount, but because I had no real income or steady employment, my options were pretty limited. I started looking in the neighborhoods that my real estate agent described variously as "up-and-coming," "transitional," and "drug- and crime-infested."

As with many other subjects, the only thing I knew about real estate was summed up in a catchphrase. In this case, it was "location, location, location." This catchphrase had been drilled into me since I was a kid because the house I grew up in was literally three doors into an upscale town with a good public school system. While many of my schoolmates' families were loaded and living in fancy hilltop houses, our neighborhood was called "the flats" and featured three types of houses with slightly varying floor plans.

"You need to buy the mediocre house in the nice neighborhood," my dad advised during our frequent phone conversations.

He had a point, but it didn't seem to pertain to me. School districts didn't matter. I wasn't handy with tools. I had no desire or money to remodel. As I saw it, the only thing I had going for me as a potential home owner was my ability to withstand excessive noise, urban eyesores, and illicit activity. I thought it would be smart to parlay these special skills into a unique investment opportunity. Let me loose in the most shitty neighborhood I could stand, and I would buy the nicest, biggest house I could afford.

When I found a house that fit the bill, a beautiful 1912 Edwardian with a renovated kitchen and bathroom, I drove past it at all hours of the day, as recommended to me by people in the know. The only crack in this otherwise sage advice was that I didn't know what I was supposed to be looking for. How bad was too bad? I had grown so accustomed to a certain level of chaos that the usual warning signs didn't stand out to me. When I pulled my car around the corner to find the cops had blocked off the street, I thought, "Cool, this house is in a neighborhood where the cops will come!" When I saw that the corner store was a magnet for teenage boys all dressed in the same clothing with the same hairstyle, I thought, "This is doable because, statistically speaking, gang members mostly just kill other gang members." Only when I walked into the store, and it turned out that the guy bragging about his Glock and his Uzi would be my next door neighbor did I get a little worried. But then he clarified to all of us standing in line that he only used his weapons on haters who fucked with his shit.

One morning during this process, I decided to park my car across the street from the house and check out the activity for a bit. In less than a minute, this same guy and an associate of his approached and motioned for me to roll down my window, which I did, mostly to demonstrate the part about me not being a hater who would remotely try to fuck with his shit. All they wanted to know was whether I was interested in smoking a blunt with them. After watching a couple drug deals and witnessing a drunk lady doing an extremely energetic Cabbage Patch in the middle of the street (until she noticed me and insisted I give her three dollars so she could buy a bottle of shoe polish), I got my dad on the horn and gave him the report: "So far so good!" Finally, I stopped driving by when I realized that, even if I were physically caught in a cross fire of bullets while there was a rape in progress on the front lawn, I was still going to make an offer on the place. A few blocks away, this house would go for almost a hundred thousand dollars more. All this research I'd been doing would pay off.

Not only did I lack savvy about location, but also "nesting" was the furthest thing from my mind. Ever since I'd graduated from high school, all I had done was continuously run in and out of wherever I was currently sleeping. For a long time, I didn't own a bed. It would never occur to me to buy an attractive soap dish or a glass brick vase. When I went over to other peoples' houses, I would be so impressed when they had their own skillet or served tea in an actual teapot. When I saw art or framed photographs on their walls, all I could think was, "Here is a person who owns a hammer."

This is why I'm fascinated by personal decorating aesthetics, by people who consciously make their space a reflection of their personalities, just like all those magazines say you should. I know people who sew their own curtains, make wallpaper out of laminated candy wrappers, and scour flea markets for antique water-spigot handles to adorn their bedposts. I do feel a little bit of relief when I step into a home that looks like a picture-perfect rendition of a Pottery Barn catalog or like it was ripped straight from the Ikea showroom floor because those people obviously don't want to think that much about decorating either. The difference is that they are at least trying to make their homes, and therefore themselves, look presentable. Honestly, I was just excited that for the first time in my life the address on my driver's license would match the one on my checks. In twelve years, it had never happened before.

Once my offer was accepted and I moved in, my neighbors could immediately tell that I wasn't one of those New-Sheriff-in-Town types—far from it. My 1966 Ford Falcon, which had a rusted-out hood and a driver's side door that was essentially made of Bondo, was always filthy. There was a pile of debris that I didn't know what to do with stacked in my driveway. Might I need it someday to fill in the garage floor, so I wouldn't have to spend too much money on concrete? My white picket fence was usually occupied by at least five teenage boys with their pants around their ankles drinking forties and yelling at passing cars. I never called the cops when they parked their hoopty cars on their lawns and jacked up the booty bass at five in the morning. I even smiled out my window as barefoot six year olds lit fireworks off of their parents' burning cigarettes and threw them on the rooftops. I thought it was important not to make waves.

It's also true that I wasn't particularly looking forward to interacting with my neighbors, but I realized I couldn't completely ignore them as I'd always done when I lived in San Francisco. This was a working-class, black neighborhood where some of the families had lived for over thirty years. Everybody made it their business to know what was going on and that scared me. The house was technically in Berkeley, which contrary to popular belief is not all wisteria-covered, communal Julia Morgan homes existing totally off the power grid with accompanying hydroponic heirloom tomato gardens. My neighborhood was a mishmash of old houses, Bauhaus apartment buildings, weedy sidewalks, and a constant flotilla of garbage blowing down the street. The other end of town, the one with the wine and cheese shops and Alice Waters' landmark restaurant Chez Panisse, was called Gourmet Ghetto. Our neighborhood, right on the Berkeley/Oakland border and characterized by a lot of government-subsidized housing, also had a nickname: Brokeley.

My strategy at first was to be really friendly. If my neighbors could see that I was a nice lady and not an evil agent of gentrification, they might accept me. Then we could move on to that next important level of race relations—ignoring one another. I said hello to anyone and everyone who passed, whether they were pushing baby strollers, smoking weed, or doing both at the same time. Most people greeted me back, so it seemed like I was doing the right thing, although sometimes there were problems. For instance, many of my neighbors spent a majority of their days and evenings sitting on their front steps. When I walked out my front door to take out the trash, they would look up, and we would wave at each other. No problem. An hour later, I would walk out the front door to go to the grocery store. We would wave again. Then I'd come back with my groceries. Same thing. All I needed were some puppets and a trolley, and I could have been mistaken for Mr. Rogers.

The other thing I had to get used to was the incessant ringing of my doorbell. It was like some sort of hazing ritual. Mostly it was people selling things, but not newspapers or cable TV connections. (Although apparently there was a guy who would pirate cable for people by shimmying up the telephone pole in front of their houses and hot-wiring them to paying customers. I *wished* he would come by.) The bell rang for the first time about three days after I moved in. It was 7:30 in the morning. I can't believe I even got out of bed to answer it, but living in a house for the first time in ages was confusing. It wasn't an apartment building. Somebody wasn't ringing the wrong buzzer; they were obviously there to talk to me. I opened the door to find a jittery lady in short shorts, a tube top, and a pair of oversized Velcro-closing tennis shoes, holding a TiVo. She wanted only five bucks for it, but I was sure if I bought it, this lady would signal all the people on her informal circuit, and I would be barraged with hot merchandise daily. It took awhile for the word to spread that I didn't put out. Until my reputation was made, I was bombarded at all hours of the day. People climbed the steps to my house and wanted to know if I had any interest in baby formula, lawn chairs, or tarps for my boat that I didn't have. Or was I interested in a gravy boat? It came with a matching creamer.

Once a woman came up to me as I was getting out of my car

and shoved a piece of paper in my face. "This is my fishing license," she said. I looked down, and there in a dirty, five-gallon bucket were three very ugly, probably mercury-filled fish, looking comatose in the gray water. "I'll give you the big one for ten dollars," she said. I tried to look impressed with the fish's size because I've heard that people who fish appreciate that, but I told her I wasn't interested in buying any today. "I'm supposed to start junior college tomorrow, and now I can't afford to buy my books!" she screamed and stomped off, water splashing out of the bucket. I stayed in the driveway and watched her as she went down to the street and took a seat on the curb. Eventually, a car pulled up, and she got in, yanking her bucket of fish angrily onto her lap. That must have been the final test because no one tried to sell me anything after I'd turned down the big fish. I did still get queried about paying for services, most often in the landscaping department.

My biggest challenge as a home owner was keeping up the yard. I had done so much yard work as a child that I was convinced of the importance of a tidy yard, yet I had neither the inclination to do it myself nor the money to pay someone else to do it for me. I would wait until it got out of control, then I'd pound a pot of coffee and try to tame this patch of wilderness with a weed whacker until I bottomed out twenty minutes into the task.

Eli wasn't any help. He hadn't officially moved in with me yet because while I was away on tour, he had signed a lease on a warehouse with a corrugated tin roof and a mosquito problem. But he who was raised in rural Arizona, playing on rocks and patches of dirt as a child, saw no benefit in a prize lawn. He didn't even seem to notice that the front of our house was a savannah of untamed weeds and brush.

I did manage to pick up the garbage that blew into our fence a few times a week, an effort fueled mainly by an interest in anthropology. There was an endless supply of candy bar wrappers, liquor bottles, blunt tips, drug baggies, and—most of all—lottery tickets. We lived three houses down from the corner store, and I figured out that that must be the exact distance it took for people to scratch off their tickets, see that they had lost, and throw it into my yard in disgust. I imagined what a hero I would be if I could just convince everyone to toss a dollar into my yard instead of a losing scratcher. I would put all the money in a coffee tin, and, at the end of the year, I would surprise everyone by buying something the whole neighborhood could enjoy, like a trampoline or a whole lot of liquor. It would be the best block party ever!

One morning I was in the corner store, and Terence, who lived across the street, made some friendly comment about how the yard was getting, as he put it, "a little deep."

This confirmed my suspicion that even the drug dealer was gossiping about my lackluster landscaping skills.

"Yeah," I said. "I've been pretty lazy about it lately."

The man in line in front of us, who was wearing a suit and tie and had left his Mercedes idling out front, reeled around and bellowed, "Well, there are some of us who cannot afford to be lazy!" I looked to Terence for some back up, but he just started laughing.

"What's so funny, young man?" he boomed. "I see you out there on the stoop all day."

Now there was no way he could accuse Terence of being lazy. Terence may have been sitting on his ass talking on his cell phone, but he was conducting a brisk business almost around the clock. But then the other man delivered the goods.

"I see you bringing our community down," he told Terence. All of a sudden, I felt like I was in a Spike Lee movie. The man turned back to me and said, "My nephew lives in this neighborhood, and he hasn't had the opportunities you've had. He would welcome a chance to earn some money mowing your lawn." Then he purchased his three airplane-sized bottles of Johnnie Walker and left.

I moved ahead in the line and ordered a piece of fried chicken. "White girl likes fried chicken!" Terence laughed and stuck out his hand for me to shake it. He had seen me, and I'm sure many other white people, eating fried chicken in his life. Still, he had to say it every time. This was fairly common. All of my neighbors liked to comment on the fact that they were black, and I was white. It was a tension breaker, I suppose, but it was hard to keep chuckling every time and saying, "Yes, I sure am white!" Obviously, I was trying to pretend that everything was normal, whereas they just decided to be up front about it.

But still, an afternoon standing around the beer cooler at my neighbor Nay Nay's house started to sound like improv night at the Laugh Factory. Whenever the cops rolled by and I was standing in between Nay Nay and her friend Pee Wee, they'd say, "Here comes the po-po! They're wondering what is up with this Oreo cookie over here!" The best comment by far came when Kobe Bryant was accused of rape, and Pee Wee was talking about how black women were down on Kobe because he only likes white women. "Is his wife white?" I asked. I'd never seen her before.

"Yeah," he said. "She's Puerto Rican or Mexican, some kind of white."

The biggest joke of all, however, was how the neighborhood really started to suffer once I moved in. "You see what happens when white people move in?" Pee Wee would say, poking me in the left side of my rib cage and then the right. "It all starts to go downhill!" He was totally right. I had to do something about that yard.

When I walked out of the store after getting my fried chicken, the man in the suit who had addressed me earlier was standing there talking to the crossing guard. I told him that if his nephew ever wanted to come over and do some yard work, I would love to pay him for it.

"Yes," he said in his deep, regal voice. "I will send him over to speak with you about it."

I'd never seen this guy before, but I knew his nephew, T. J. He was a sweetheart, about nine years old, and would come over to our house sometimes to hang out. Mostly he just wanted to jam out on Eli's bass and eat our cookies. One day I was out in the backyard picking up the rotting plums that had fallen from our tree. There were hundreds of them in various states of decay, and it probably would have taken me an hour to pick them all up. T. J. saw me and came over to ask what I was doing. I thought of his uncle and told him that if he wanted to finish up, I would pay him five bucks. He picked up a couple and then told me that he really had to go home to go to the bathroom.

The entire winter passed, and when early spring came around, the front yard was beginning to look like a jungle. The "lawn" was knee-high in some patches and up to my waist in others. A thicket of crab grass had starting climbing up one side of the house, and dandelions were springing up from the cracks in the driveway like a field of lollipops. I started to get a mental block about dealing with it, almost like a superstition. It was as if a wizard had appeared in a dream and told me that the weeds represented tenacity, and if I got rid of them, the house would start to fall apart (or something like that). It reminded me of this old hippie I had met in Santa Cruz ten years earlier who had OCD and thought cutting off his beard was bad luck. I felt powerless against the unrelenting explosion of green-ery, like I couldn't mess with its mojo.

And then one day, in an act that was either a sign from the universe or else a sign that there actually was a television crew from a makeover show in my overgrown bushes, there was a knock on my door. I opened the screen and saw a tall, skinny guy, about sixty years old, wearing a long-sleeved, flannel shirt, black jeans, and work boots in the 80-degree heat. He shook my hand, introduced himself as Wallace, and asked me if I would pay him to mow my lawn.

"Oh God, yes!" I told him. Like most visitors to my house, he appeared to be drunk, but he seemed capable of operating light machinery. "The only thing is, you have to find a lawn mower because mine was stolen, and my weed whacker broke last year."

"That will be no problem," he slurred. And then he mumbled something about a friend he had up the street at the flea market and left.

The afternoon went on, and when he didn't come back, I didn't think much about it. People were always appearing and disappearing from this block. About three hours later, I went outside to get in my car, and I saw something out of the corner of my eye. A figure. A figure buried deep in the grass. I tiptoed over and saw that it was Wallace, on his hands and knees, cutting my grass practically blade by blade with a pair of pruning shears. He had done about a two-foot square surface so far. I approached him gingerly.

"Oh, hey," I said. "I am so sorry, but you can't be . . . I mean, I can't have you . . . if I had known you were out here, I would have . . . wow."

I thought of all my neighbors looking over at my house for the last three hours. The only white lady on the block and there's a drunk, black man crawling around on his hands and knees in my front yard. I was going to get a lot of shit for this.

He paused for a second, took a sip from the tall boy can he had nestled inside a paper bag, and then started yelling. "You said you would pay me to cut the grass! You said you would pay me ten dollars!"

We actually hadn't talked about a price, but that probably would have been fair. I was impressed that he didn't go spiraling out of control, that he kept the price reasonable. The lawn, although tall, was pretty tiny. With a lawn mower, it would have taken about fifteen minutes.

"Listen, I'll give you five dollars for what you've done so far, okay?" When he didn't answer, I got down on my knees and looked him in the eye. He was covered in sweat. "Listen. Wallace. Is it okay if I give you five dollars for this little patch you've done?"

I should have just given him ten and let him go, but I was broke and had a chip on my shoulder about being ripped off.

"No!" he yelled, trying to get to his feet. "I've been working all afternoon! You told me ten dollars, and you're going to pay me my ten dollars!"

This attracted the attention of nearly everyone on the block who, if they hadn't noticed him when he was in stealth mode, could now look over and see me being threatened by a man recklessly waving around a pair of pruning shears.

"Ten dollars! Ten dollars!" Wallace insisted.

Oh, no. Here came the cracked out guy whose kids lived across the street. This guy would come and go over the months, appearing sober sometimes and deeply fucked up at others. Right now he was wasted with a capital WAY. And he was running toward us.

"Ten dollars!" The whites of his eyes were solidly yellow. "Let us do it!" he said. "I'll get all my kids, and we can do it!" Four kids between the ages of five and ten followed him.

"Can you get your hands on a lawn mower?" I asked him. "I will definitely let you do it if you can find a lawn mower."

He said he didn't have a lawn mower, but came up with another solution. "Do you got any more of those scissors?" he said. "My kids can do it faster than his tired old ass!"

Wallace was offended. "Fuck you, motherfucker! I was here first!"

Thank God, Nay Nay came walking toward us. "What is going on over here, people?"

Nay Nay is my favorite neighbor. I can't tell how old she is, somewhere between forty and sixty, with a mop of jheri curls the same color orange as her brand new Mazda RX-7. When I first moved in, she walked right up to me and gave me the run-down on who lived where and what their story was. She often brings me Budweisers, and I'll sit and listen to her bitch about her long hours working full-time as a home health care attendant and part-time as a cook at her cousin's restaurant. Nay Nay knows everything about everybody and freaks out all the kids with her constant haranguing. "Who are you?" she'll yell to an eight-year-old riding by on his bike. "Does your mama know where you're at? What's your name? What are you doing all the way down here?"

Just the sight of the neighborhood busybody coming over to bust them made everybody on my lawn take off down the street.

"Oh, man," I said to her. "That sucked!"

Nay Nay looked me in the eye and said, "Let me tell you something, girl. Those people? Those people are crazy."

"Yeah," I said, "I just thought maybe somebody could—"

She interrupted, "Listen to me now. You don't got to be talking to everybody just 'cause they be walking by. Around here, people are gonna try to make their problems your problem." She was in full lecture mode now, pointing her finger in my face.

"Well, I—"

"Hold you tongue; hold you tongue now! All I'm saying is don't let your guard down just 'cause you're standing on your own lawn!"

I thought I'd already learned that lesson years ago with the knife incident, but apparently I had to learn it again.

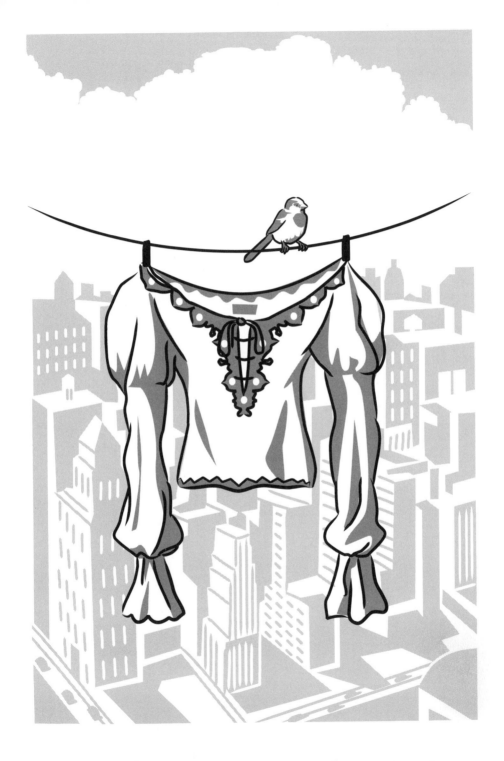

⑩ CIRCLING THE WAGONS

I am visiting New York City, and it is the season of the Peasant Look. I walk the streets of my brother Chris's SoHo neighborhood, trying not to get smothered by a billowing sleeve or garroted by a stray leather choker, when the realization hits me: By the time I return home to San Francisco in two weeks, this gauzy reign of fashion terror will only be starting to heat up there. The New York-to-San Francisco trend lapse, a period of about two weeks and holding steady, used to be much longer way back in the mid-nineties before the advent of Webcams, blogs, and that ubiquitously referenced PBS documentary on professional cool hunters. (Cool hunters are the new rocket scientists, right? As in, "It doesn't take a cool hunter to figure out if that Hooters T-shirt is ironic" or "You can learn to program your VCR. It's not cool hunting or anything." Even my mom's Monday bridge group knows what a cool hunter is, and believe me, those ladies are far less hip than the Friday group, the one with the retired elementary schoolteachers who occasionally enjoy a glass of white Zin with their Chex mix.)

So while the two-week bicoastal rule is holding steady, something that's definitely on the wane (besides cheap shot references to crack such as "Are you on crack??" and "Jesus! Lay off the crack pipe!") is the time it takes for the latest trend to make it from the streets of New York to the malls of America. As I watch a sophisticated, urban waif perusing the juice selection at Dean and Deluca, it makes me drool with pleasure to know that in about one month, thirteen-year-old girls from Bakersfield to Bangor will be removing their retainers to vomit in junior high bathrooms, wearing blouses with similar earth-toned embroidery and gathered pouf shoulders.

Let's talk about the difference between keeping it simple and "keeping it simple." Just ask Marie Antoinette, who once commissioned a play called *Les Petits Trianons* so she could step into the role of an unassuming country milkmaid, blazing a fashion trail that was basically the precursor to grunge. Peasant as a fashion choice is, of course, nothing new, but it's also something that never left the Bay Area in the first place. How can it be back when it's been here all along? From the Haight Ashbury to Telegraph Avenue in Berkeley and inside every Volkswagen or hybrid car on the bridge in between, the Bay Area is the world's petri dish for not only peasants, but also gypsies, urchins, wood nymphs, and Middle Earth druids.

We breed them here, spritz them with essential oils, and ship them off to places like women's colleges and Canada.

Maybe I'm spoiled, but I will only accept a hand-crocheted doo rag when it's worn on the head of a suburban runaway with dirty feet spare-changing me as she fries her tits off on acid. You should only earn the freedom to rock a stained piano shawl slung around your hips when you're also hawking funky, grayish-brown, handmade soap in front a used bookstore, not when you're working in the publishing industry and getting regular facials. But by polishing this turd, these fashionistas, these legions of well-groomed, New York women working a look described in the print of their glossy bibles as "lyrical!" and "folkloric!" are about as earthy as Raelian-sect space clones. If they'd at least appear as if they were enjoying their collective lyrical moment, I might be able to raise a glass to their uncanny ability to follow the step-by-step instructions in *Elle's* "Get This Look!" section. Instead, they breeze past wearing an expression of self-congratulation on making it through a whole day without eating wheat. Or perhaps they are reflecting on a particularly riveting Bikram class. The mystique of the farmer's daughter is really lost when I know full well there's a fresh Brazilian bikini wax underneath each and every one of those macramé slouch belts.

I had just drifted out of my reverie to use my X-ray vision on a model type in a three-tiered, peach, lace, prairie skirt when— whoa!—here comes a nineteenth-century Moldavian prostitute. Oh wait, it's just Cameron Diaz. As usual, she's one step ahead of the pack, this time by fully integrating the tweed newsboy cap, whose D-day for San Francisco at that time must have been at least six weeks away. That's why Cam can sashay along with extra pride and confidence. She knows she's got this trend to herself for awhile. She knows deep inside that my nine-year-old niece in Carol Stream, Illinois, won't be buying the nine-dollar version of that hat from the Delia's catalog for at least another two months. *You're not just the newsboy, lady. You're the news!* I turn to watch her slink down Broadway, and then I head back to my brother's place, counting the number of jeans with preworn butts that I see along the way. I imagine these girls, wrestling with their cigarette lighters and Gucci sunglasses, being hog-tied and pulled through ye olde towne square like heathens. *I just came in from a sample sale, and boy is my ass tired!*

A loft. In SoHo. It sounds either fabulously fancy or disconcertingly upscale, depending on my mood. I'm sure that's because all of my New York friends either live in Brooklyn or spend half the year playing fretless bass in a cover band on a cruise ship, so they can afford their tiny Lower East Side studios. Lord knows I jumped at the chance to house-sit in luxury's lap. Mildly disheveled and smelling like beer, I arrive at Chris and my sister-in-law Lora's place just as they are zipping shut their matching black Tumi suitcases and heading off on their honeymoon to the Amalfi Coast in Italy.

Both of them work in advertising, and they met on the job. Despite a few industry setbacks—9/11, the economy, and K-Mart's failed attempts to turn the Blue Light (of Blue Light Special fame) into a cuddly animated icon that kids would love, like Tony the Tiger—they are doing pretty well for themselves. My brother and I earn the same amount of money, in a way. It's just that it takes me a month to achieve his day rate. In other words, at the end of a workday, having sketched out some slogans for a new brand of energy water or presented a boardroom full of Lexus strategy people with a new teaser campaign, Chris has earned my take-home pay for an entire month.

I used to think that I could do this kind of work—that almost anyone with a good haircut and some nice shoes could. I would picture myself perched on the edge of someone's desk with a notebook, thinking outside the box, shifting the paradigm, moving the needle, brainstorming fresh ideas for a bold, new product targeted at single mothers on the go. Then one day, in the depths of my financial distress, I sincerely tried to visualize myself arguing about a toaster strudel's "yum factor." Could I get excited about the life-changing potential in a dryer sheet? Could I deal with the karmic fallout of hijacking Tom Waits's "Rain Dogs" for an Alpo commercial? And that's when I started to really respect Chris and Lora. Day after day, they jump into the great American mosh pit where art meets commerce and emerge with a big, dirty paycheck. One of Lora's favorite expressions, often uttered when returning home with a clutch of shopping bags or signing her credit card receipt after treating me to a hundred-dollar sushi lunch, is "I need to get rid of the dirty ad money!"

I think they're worth every penny. Chris, after all, is responsible for writing the Taco Bell Chihuahua's catchphrase of yore, "Drop the chalupa!"—a fact that has been the source of pride in our family for years. While my parents usually get stumped trying to explain any modicum of achievement on my behalf, Chris is easy.

There was a time, in our early twenties, when it almost looked as if I was going to be the respectable one. It seems hard to believe, considering I had lost all my hair in a bleaching accident and was making eight dollars an hour as a baker while shacking up with a boyfriend who made paintings of dogs wearing those long cones around their necks to keep them from biting themselves. Chris was having something of an identity crisis after dropping out of West Point. Ever since he was a toddler, he had believed he was going to be a career military man, but two years into college, the reality of taking classes like Terrain Analysis or Small Unit Tactics and marching in a square for hours in the snow as punishment for having scuffed shoes set in. He "acted out" for a few years after that, which included, but was scarcely limited to, the purchase of an Alfa Romeo with questionable funds and repeated attempts to create a paycheck at the craps tables in Reno.

When Chris decided he wanted to get into advertising, most people his age in that business already had a few years of experience under their belts. But he got serious. One afternoon he put on a white turtleneck sweater, walked into a piano showroom, and had himself photographed with a smug look on his face while seated at a white baby grand. Then he went to our childhood friend Amy, now a graphic designer, and had her create a tri-fold laminated resume that charted the milestones in his life next to that of another man who was also pictured wearing a white turtleneck and smugly seated at a white baby grand. That man was then *Entertainment Tonight* co-host and fledgling New Age musician John Tesh. The resume showed that while Tesh was courting television actress Connie Selleca, Chris was being dumped by child psychology major Lindsay Glickman. While Tesh was releasing his album, *Sax by the Fire*, Chris was being chastised for not wearing regulation trousers at a restaurant called D.B.A. O'Lafferty's. My brother was immediately hired by a large San Francisco agency and quickly moved up the ladder to jobs in Los Angeles and finally New York.

I may have performed at a festival called Homo-a-Go-Go with legendary transgender activist Kate Bornstein while wearing bifocals and a man wig, but Chris invented a popular fast-food chain catchphrase that delighted millions of people in their homes, multiple times on a nightly basis. My parents once called me in a state of frenzy because they had been watching Monday Night Football when John Madden quipped, "It looks like Rice dropped the chalupa on that one!" My dad's voice got all high-pitched as he sputtered, "This thing is huge! It's in the consciousness of the American people!" I briefly considered starting a support group with the siblings of the "Where's the Beef?" and the "Got Milk?" guys. I will admit a certain amount of satisfaction when Taco Bell dropped the dog, not to mention Chris's agency, and he started working on

Pilsner Urquell beer. It had been around forever, but I guarantee nobody in my family had ever heard of it before. Basically, Pilsner Urquell was the Kate Bornstein of lagers.

But back to my brother's loft in SoHo. The Lincoln Town Car has been waiting downstairs for twenty minutes, but Chris and Lora don't seem to be in a rush. She carefully selects travel-size bottles of Kiehl's skin care products and places them in her carry-on, while he removes some unnecessary receipts from his buttery leather wallet and drops them in a Prada shopping bag under his desk. I observe their affluent newlywed-ness with a mixture of affection and anthropological curiosity.

I'm particularly intrigued by my own physical changes in their presence. How strange that my BO gets worse when I'm around them. My teeth become more yellowed, my skin more blotchy. It's as if my unappealing traits were stepping up to fight for their lives in a world where Crest Whitestrips are precious enough to sit in locked drugstore display cases next to the razor blades. All the crow's feet and upper lip hairs, defensive about being permanently phased out of visible society, want to stand up and be counted. This is what happens with prolonged exposure to the alpha-groomed, those people who transform everyone around them into beings more stippled, flaky, toxic, hunched. My T-zone has never been as oily as it is under the alabaster sconces that hang from their eighteen-foot ceilings. In their presence, I can almost hear my gums receding.

A box of hazelnut biscotti lies open on the coffee table, and, as

I crunch into one, sending a spray of crumbs into my lap, I notice the piedmont of unopened wedding gifts on the floor around the dining room table. Tiny Barneys foothills covered with clusters of Tiffany's boxes dotting them like bright blue wildflowers. I have never been to Tiffany's. I have never been to Barneys. It's mostly because I'm always broke, hate to shop, and have a deeply schizophrenic fashion sense that I'm too disinterested in to cure.

There was a time when I thought I knew fashion. I had a semblance of personal style, predicated on my five-dollar rule. If something cost under five dollars and I had never seen anything like it before, I would buy it, no matter what size or how fucked up it was. I bought bright green golf pants in a size 14, tiny kids shirts with elementary school logos, vintage dresses cut for women with no hips, and bloomers with questionable stains. I operated as if imbued with some special sixth sense that instilled in me the power to recognize the potential in every swatch of unnatural fiber, no matter how smelly or pilled. I was immediately drawn to things I thought looked good, but not necessarily things that looked good *on*.

A few years ago, I saw a picture of myself that put the wheels in motion for a wardrobe upheaval. I was at a reception for a photography show where the subjects were all spoken-word performers in San Francisco. The photos were very similar to one another in that they were all black and white portraits of people standing onstage behind a microphone. They also shared the unfortunate characteristic of showing everyone with his or her face horribly contorted into the usual assortment of unattractive expressions that go along with being captured mid-word. It wasn't my heavily shadowed fright mask or the glint of spit on my lower lip that freaked me out, however. My outfit was committing even worse offenses than my eyes, which appeared crossed, like I was trying to read my poem off a grain of rice that was stuck to the mic stand. In the photo, my right knee jutted skyward, and my upper body was arching back. The darts in my early 1960s blouse were woefully unfilled, giving my boobs the appearance of collapsed Sno-Kone cups. My puce-colored Sta-Prest Wranglers had such a long crotch that with my leg kicking up like that, it appeared as if I was packing a fully erect, ten-inch dick. What was I doing? Why didn't anybody say something?

I slowly began to curb my thrift store shopping, but it was a tough habit to break. Besides the price factor, I liked knowing that the only other person alive with my same green and yellow, checkered, wool vest was probably a sixty-year-old lady who worked the register at a mom-and-pop auto repair shop in southern Michigan. It was fun to think about who owned that baby blue Windbreaker before me, to make up a story about them. Even though I eventually acquired a pretty low-maintenance uniform of old corduroys, T-shirts, and one pair of shoes, the fact remains: To this day, and it shames me to admit it, I have a basement full of stained, ripped, buttonless, broken-zippered, ill-fitting, one-of-a-kind items, most of them moldering in plastic garbage bags. They're vintage! To my estimation, I am sure I own at least fifty dresses, a hundred T-shirts with various stupid logos or messages, thirty jackets, twenty-five skirts, forty sweaters, not to mention pantsuits, kimonos, bathing suits, halter tops, slips, hats, and ugly, uncomfortable, scuffed, second-hand shoes, none of which I wear.

My real weakness, however, has always been pants. I am a pants lady. I finally had a garage sale last summer and sold twenty-five pairs, mostly to the same girl from Brooklyn on her way to Burning Man. She was so stoked that she gave me her phone number and told me to call her next time I was in town. And I still probably have about a hundred pairs of pants in my basement.

The pace at the loft is picking up as the driver of the Lincoln Town Car rings the bell for the third time, yelling that he's going to leave if Chris and Lora don't appear soon. To me, this is a shining example of what it's like when you have money. You can have almost anything you want exactly when you want it. The streets are crawling with other cars for them to hire, and they know it. My brother adjusts his platinum wedding ring and then casually pulls a cashmere crewneck over his head. I can barely remember the dorky adolescent who had the collection of wildly colorful, acrylic sweaters to rival the mid-eighties Bill Cosby. He has joined the Tasteful Nation, becoming conscious about clean lines, luxury fabrics, and updated classics. I walk them out to the elevator, they hand me the keys, and then Lora utters the words that really matter: "Feel free to wear any of my clothes," she says. "Anything in the closet is yours."

The elevator doors close, I walk back into the apartment, taking in the wall of windows looking out on Wooster Street. From there it's approximately fifteen to twenty seconds before I fling open the double doors of the closet, stand back, and take a good look. Arranged neatly, although not anally, are fifteen solid feet of chic, upscale clothing, mostly by hip designers with boutiques in the neighborhood. These are the not the bland uniforms of the conservative rich or the tacky expenditures of the tasteless. As I run my hand along the silk, the wool, the leather, the sassy tops with hand-stitching, the dresses with funky matching belts and piles of little sweaters, I realize that if I were rich, and I got over that hump that poor people who suddenly come into money always talk about—the point when suddenly they are able to say, "I deserve it, damn it!"—these are probably some of the exact clothes I would buy.

The shoe racks tower above me displaying a collection of fifty pairs strong and overwhelmingly favoring Prada, Miu Miu, and Marc Jacobs. I slip off my well-worn black Fluevogs, an eighty-dollar purchase that felt extravagant until I ended up wearing them every single day for two years, and slide my calloused toes into a pair of Prada snakeskin, strappy sandals. I try to walk around the room, lifting up the hems of my corduroys to check myself out in the full-length mirror. Wow. If I thought I was out of my element in this loft before, just looking down at my gnarly feet in these delicate little sandals really gave new meaning to the term "bull in the china shop." I don't have a rich person's feet. It's too late for that. I put the heels back, shut the doors, and decide to turn off the lights, sit on the couch, and spy on the neighbor for awhile. When I see him stretching a canvas, I let out a sigh of relief knowing there are still artists left in the neighborhood. But on closer inspection, I realize he is just smoothing a duvet across a maple sleigh bed.

The next morning, I actually attempt to wear my own clothes. I open my suitcase and pull out a pair of cords, but the closet is beckoning. Just a pair of pants, I think. Let's see what a pair of fancy pants feels like. When faced with such a huge selection, I decide the best strategy is simply to pull the top pair off the stack. They're brown, denim-like, slightly bootcut, slightly low-rise, but I swear that when I put these pants on, it is a revelation. There is no weird bunching around my thighs or crotch, no excess fabric around my waist. They are not too tight in the hips. The placement of the back pockets doesn't make my ass look weirdly elongated or give the optical illusion that my butt has been compressed in a horizontal tube. These pants fit me perfectly. It's like when you have your first taste of good coffee or good beer, or you get a ride in a car that has leather upholstery, or you sleep on high-thread-count hotel sheets.

For the next two weeks, I wear those pants every single day. I consider trying on some others, but I've done so well already. Why push it? I feel better knowing that perhaps there is one perfect pair of pants in the world, but I probably couldn't handle knowing that there are more. Some days I start out putting on a pair of my own, but they immediately make me feel like either a clown or an inmate. Even if a pair of these nice pants costs fifty dollars, I'll buy them, I think. I'm committed enough to go that deep. I look up the address of the boutique on the label, and it just so happens to be right around the corner from the loft. Of course it is. (The only thing you can buy just around the corner from my place is crack. For weed, you can just go next door.)

It's a small shop, completely unpretentious, and I feel myself understanding their stripped-down yet accessible aesthetic. This is the New York boutique that, probably without much thought, has been marketed to someone exactly like me. The merchandise is folded, but not too uniformly, and there's plenty of it around. It's not one of those stores with five things in two colors. There is no stupid music blaring. It sounds like the girl in back is listening to a CD of her friend's band, most likely a mildly successful indie rock outfit whose lead singer is in his late thirties, has a master's in poetry, and lives in the Midwest with his wife, a fiction writer or college professor. There's only one other woman shopping, and when I hear the owner say, "Here you go, Parker," I look and realize that it is indeed Parker Posey. That's it. I'm upping my ante to a hundred dollars. I can put a hundred dollars on my card.

I try not to stare, but something about her looks a little off. I always thought that if I saw Parker Posey on the street, she would look a little sloppy, maybe wearing a hooded sweatshirt and a down vest, casually ordering coffee at a deli and picking lint off the change in her pocket. I always thought, like any other thirty-four-year-old mom with a rich fantasy life who thinks the world is held together by the wind that blows through Christopher Guest's hair, that it would be nice to have Parker Posey's career—a respectable paycheck, good scripts, the braces, the cheerleading moves.

But when I sneak a peek at her out of the corner of my eye, I see that today she is rocking the peasant look. Hard. It's so peasant, it's almost Ren Faire. Maybe she's researching a role, I think optimistically. I plunk down my pants, noticing she has just bought the exact same pair. As $161 gets rung up, I hand over my card, amazed at the Parker in me.

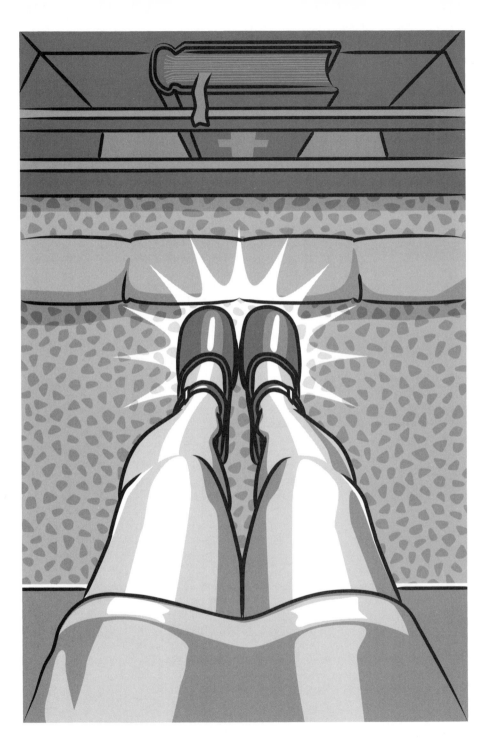

THE LOWLY HUSTLE

Ladies and gentlemen, let's hear it for "The Apostles' Creed"!

I remember sitting with my family at the Church of the Sacred Heart, Sunday morning mass, getting revved up for my favorite prayer. Only moments before, I'd been in pure preteen, spaced-out mode, watching the dust move through the air in the refracted light from the stained glass, pausing a second to think how much of that dust was actually getting stuck to my thick coat of lip gloss, karate-chopping my hand in front of my face to break up the slow-moving school of particles, and then, showtime! I'd stand up and cock my left hip out a little. It was time to pray.

Even the second graders knew the "Our Father" by heart. "The Hail Mary," with its complete lack of gravitas, didn't even rank. I felt sorry for Mary, after all she'd gone through and that was her prayer. On the one hand, "The Hail Mary" seemed to me like the "Row, Row, Row Your Boat" of Catholic prayers, something that you might be able to jazz up by doing in a round at a slumber party, but would never compete with making the popular girl levitate. "The Apostles' Creed," on the other hand, was solo material, obviously waiting for the right person to take it by the horns. And I was sure that person was me.

Just in case someone was sifting through the chorus of voices to listen specifically to mine (which seemed entirely possible to me at the time) and that someone (a strange, older man perhaps) took an interest in how I was reciting my prayers, I wanted to make sure that I exuded a slightly bored quality. *He was crucified, died, and was buried. He shall come again to judge the living and the dead. And his kingdom shall have no end.* I thought it accented my total and complete memorization nicely. Bored, but without missing a beat. That was the desired effect. If any of the two hundred members of the congregation looked over, they could see a twelve-year-old girl going totally commando on The Creed, sans misselette. I figured if I memorized it, I was then free to forget it was even happening to me. I became a soldier—a soldier who was then put on furlough to slack off and fantasize about a world in which it just might be possible to have a perm for half of the week and straight hair the other half.

It was around this time that a product called Party Perm hit the market, which supposedly made this precise fantasy possible. To claim divine intervention—"I was in Church, and God answered my prayer"—is a tad melodramatic. I do believe, however, that Party Perm's invention may have been the result of the concentrated hope emanating from a critical mass of girls and women at the time, as well as a few select men (including Mr. Julian, the band teacher who drove one of those midget campers called a Chinook and showed up one Monday with a perm that mysteriously disappeared by Thursday).

I imagined the breakthrough happening as follows:

INT: Clairol laboratory. Two attractive female scientists take a break by a vending machine. Amanda, a bubbly Midwesterner with a wild mane of red, curly hair, chats with Ellen, a more reserved professional with straight, blond hair.

AMANDA: [*ripping open an energy bar, back when they were called granola bars and trail mix was called GORP*] Your hair is so pretty, Ellen. I wish I could have straight hair. Well, sometimes.

ELLEN: [*pouring hot water over her Mug-a-Lunch, a precursor to Cup Noodles*] Really? That's so funny because I often think about how fun it would be to have curly hair. Not all the time, you see, just some of the time.

[*Graphic of lightning bolt simulating the accumulated energy of all world citizens having this same thought, including the seventh grader in the Gunne Sax dress reciting "The Apostles' Creed," which then morphs into light bulbs over the heads of Amanda and Ellen.*]

AMANDA: Bingo!
ELLEN: Let's get to work, sister!
[*End scene*]

There were always a few sullen kids, skulking and hungover, who refused to say the prayer at all. Their parents pretended not to notice. I had heard of something called "teenage rebellion" when watching 60 *Minutes* with my parents, but that couldn't be it, could it? I didn't know any of these rebels personally, but I was fairly sure that rebellion didn't come cloaked in wide-wale corduroys, top-siders with the laces fashioned into little coils, and an oxford shirt that Mom ironed for them that morning before they slid into the backseat of the Buick Park Avenue, put their seat belts on, and went to Church. Rebellion had to look better than that.

If any of my peers had seen the segment with Morley Safer on the weekly news magazine and were planning on rebelling, they had better pick up the slack and go all-out because there was no way I was jumping on that bandwagon. I knew that much. For starters, my mom had left a Reese's Peanut Butter Cup waiting for me on the butcher's block in the kitchen when I got home from school every single day for seven years, and it didn't look like she was going to let up any time soon. I also got to glue corkboard onto an entire wall of my bedroom and pick out my own bedspread from the JCPenney catalog. I'd have been crazy to give up that kind of life. So I had to come to Church here and breeze through "The Apostles' Creed" once a week, so what. It's only Church, I wanted to tell all my fellow adolescents who were having trouble accepting Christ as their personal savior. It would only hurt you if you actually believed.

I loved standing shoulder to shoulder with my brothers, watching all those dry Sunday morning mouths droning on and on while the monsignor glared at everybody and Jesus, all sinewy, shiny, and tan, hanged on the cross behind him. I would creep myself out so easily by focusing on a nail in Jesus' hand, then blinking, focusing on the foamy, white gunk at the corner of someone's mouth, then blinking, focusing on an old lady's arthritic claw gnarled around a rosary, and then blinking. The crown of thorns. Blink. Smoke rising from the crucible. Blink. A major case of neck acne in front of you. Blink. The blood of the lamb. Blink. With all those personalized jump cuts and a backing track of chanting zombies doing the Creed, it was a little like making my own Klaus Kinksi movie.

But my very favorite thing to do in Church was to position the toes of my shoes to stick out from the front edge of the kneeler when I stood up. Then I would look down at them, concentrate, and try to imagine what kind of shoes I would have in the future. For instance, what shoes would I be wearing next week? And more specifically, what set of actions and circumstances would occur in the next week to make me put on that pair of shoes that morning? It was *The Butterfly Effect* as writ in tween footwear. Maybe I would break my leg and have a cast, I thought optimistically. I could lose a toe, who knew. When I looked down thirty-nine weeks from then or one-hundred-and-seventy-two Sundays in the future, what would have just happened to me? Would I be rich? Would I be pretty? Would I have forty-five dollars in my pocket because I just dressed up as a giant banana and handed out free bananas to office workers in a downtown San Francisco plaza while dancing to the song "Celebration," while my husband and two-year-old son were at the flea market buying discount tube socks as a surprise present for me? Anything could happen in this life. The world was full of possibilities. . . .

It was a banner week, the one that ended with me crouching behind a fire truck in an alley trying to squeeze a spongy banana suit over my ass. I'd already made $60 at a focus group for a new brand of "clear spirits" (which tasted like carbonated Flintstone vitamins) on Monday, sold off my partial collection of ratty thrift store coats for $55 on Tuesday, appeared in a low-budget commercial for a chain of check-cashing stores for $150 on Thursday, and now this: an hour and a half in the suit for $45. All I had to do was stop by the *Coin-Star* machine and dump in the loot from those shoe boxes in my closet, and I could clear over $375 this week. I was like a college student designing my own major, except I was thirty-five and designing my own minimum wage temp job.

I had recently run into my old friend Chris, who had worked with me at the weekly newspaper ten years before. Back then I was a receptionist, and he was the assistant to the lady who sold advertising to booksellers and publishing companies. We both wanted to be writers. I remember being slightly envious to see him return to the office after a meeting with a used bookstore manager, clutching their latest ad in his hand. I'd think, "Wow, he just had lunch with the manager of an actual bookstore. His writing career is really taking off." Chris went on to publish a few stories, but with the ballooning dot-com economy, he decided to start his own business called The Fruit Guys. The Fruit Guys delivered fresh fruit to offices and was a perfect addition to those San Francisco workplaces that already had their own chocolate Labrador puppies, air hockey tables, and free screenings for human papillomavirus (i.e., warts). If anyone needed to enjoy a crisp, organic Bosc pear from the comfort of their ergonomic workstation in the year 2000, it was these people.

Chris could tell I wasn't doing too well financially. Maybe the tip-off was the way I eyed his double latte like it was a Bulgari watch and shifted nervously as he brought the cup to his lips, as if to say, "You're just going to whip that out on the street? In front of everyone?" He told me there were occasional opportunities to work for his company at promotional events, like the one this coming Friday, but I would have to "wear the suit"—a giant foam banana costume.

It seemed too obvious to feel humiliated, so I immediately nipped that shame spiral in the bud by switching to another tactic altogether. I thought about how much I've always loved mascots, and how only bitter people with dark, angry hearts didn't. It made me so happy to hug a gorilla at the mall or shake hands with a squishy caulking gun at the hardware store. They were people, just like anybody else, doing their jobs, having good days, really owning their characters, flirting with grandmas, or busting out with some unsolicited air saxophone on a lark. And they had bad days, on which they refused to pose for photographs with babies or yelled muffled threats through their mesh breathing holes.

I found the quality and craftsmanship of their outfits fascinating, too. I was always honing in on the loose threads and scuffed vinyl, seeing what kind of shoes the character chose to wear. I once saw a computer in a pair of slip-on Vans, which was so perfect: a casual computer who might go skateboarding later. But then there was the ice cream cone in flip flops. I don't think anyone wants to see rough, cracked heels, and crooked toes sticking out of the bottom of a waffle cone. I started to come around to the idea that if there was anybody who would know what it takes to bring an inanimate object to life on a short-term promotional assignment in a public space, it was me. I'd been doing unofficial research for years.

Having given myself the psychological and financial pep talk that enabled me to accept the job, I was immediately seized by a familiar feeling. It's the same one I got when I did readings at outdoor festivals and street fairs. There people would be trying to enjoy an Amstel Lite or a corn dog, and little did they know they were stepping into harm's way via an open air poetry reading. All they wanted to do was get their jazz on or browse through the selection of painted gourds, or, if it was a different kind of street fair, get spanked or do a whip-it, but there it was: a loud, annoying voice they couldn't block out or escape. At the makeshift *biergarten* and the hemp booth, by the kettle corn barrel, and in the Porta Potties, broadcasting from a stage six blocks away and reverberating off of buildings throughout the neighborhood, this voice had often been my voice. I know that people who book outdoor poetry readings have good intentions, but pretty much everyone orating out in the elements with a crappy microphone and no monitor is going to sound like a nut job the minute you're not standing directly in front of them watching their lips move. It was like Stockholm Syndrome in reverse. I sympathized with the people I was hurting with my words.

In much the same way, my stint in the banana suit was going to hurt people—I knew that. At noon on Friday, many people were going to take one look at this thirty-five-year-old mom with broken capillaries on her nose, bad posture, and worn out soles on her shoes, dressed as a giant banana, and it was going to fill them with pity for me. At least I could count on others to be so broken, so spent by the end of the week, that they would just be thrilled to get a free banana in the middle of their workday. I decided that if my plans for having a positive attitude went south, I could always keep the chain of sadness going by taking pity on them.

I showed up at the plaza ten minutes before I was supposed to meet Chris, which is what people who have not had steady work in a long time often do. Get there early! Got a job to do! Step aside,

I'm working today! I'd been told that the banana looked best when worn with black pants, a long-sleeved black shirt and black shoes, so that's what I wore in the 95-degree heat, psyching myself up as I desperately sought out shade. "This is going to be hilarious," I said over and over like a mantra, until I caught my reflection in a wall of windows and saw how distorted my face looked from all the jaw clenching.

I'd also found an old pair of Ray Ban knockoffs at home and brought those along, so I could be a Cool Banana. I loved how the addition of sunglasses to anything instantly made it cool—a signifier, as it is called in fields of study I no longer know anything about. Sunglasses = cool. Who started that? Snoopy? Often I'll see a cartoon sun wearing sunglasses, like "Hey, don't worry about your friend the sun! He's cool!" Then of course there's a certain personality type that indiscriminately slaps sunglasses on dogs and babies, two of the most uncool creatures on earth.

I was hoping the costume allowed me to have a hand free, so I could do that thing where you slide your sunglasses down the bridge of your nose and look out over them while raising your eyebrows. If anybody wanted to photograph me, I planned on that being my signature pose—the same pose every time. I wanted it to be like when you see pictures of William Shatner or the Queen of England. No matter whom they're standing next to, what the weather is like, or what decade it is, they're always looking eerie and wax-like, striking the same pose, their mouths forming the same smile. Flipping through their personal photo albums, slowly scanning page after page, photo after photo of them looking exactly the same in every one, must feel like being perpetually trapped in the climax scene of a psychological thriller.

I surveyed my surroundings. There were two rows of tents and booths set up, and the whole thing had a tedious, informational feel—as if the event coordinator was actually a robot who had been mentored by a pamphlet. It appeared to be some kind of health-consciousness-raising fair, something about hearts and lungs. No balloons, no cotton candy, but because it was San Francisco, there was of course a freak on a star-spangled unicycle. Not that this guy had any official affiliation with the proceedings; he just pretended he did to finagle more tips into his hat—which was, predictably, a tall stovepipe with a black-and-white Holstein cow pattern. (If sunglasses = cool, Holstein cow pattern = fun.)

At that moment, I was merely an outsider lurking on a planter box, dressed entirely in soft, black clothing among the muted tones of the business casual uniforms, looking like a mime gearing up for her greasepaint or perhaps just a stagehand on a smoke break. But when I mentally switched to an aerial view of the setting, I could see the future. In just a few minutes, amid the slow-moving foot traffic and sea of paper bag lunchers, there would be a lone banana, bright yellow and deceptively earnest, weaving through the crowd.

I looked up and saw Chris's business partner striding across the plaza in khakis and a polo shirt emblazoned with the company's logo, which depicted two laborers heaving an oversized pear rendered in the style of WPA mural art. The logo made me feel like I was part of something big, a movement of some kind. He picked up a walkie-talkie and reported my arrival to the other end, as Chris's Volvo station wagon, laden with dozens of bunches of bananas, rolled up the street. I peeked in the back window. Draped over the bananas, like an emperor riding in on a litter of his minions, was my banana suit.

"Get me into this baby!" I said, actually rubbing my palms together to appear as enthusiastic as possible. I was experienced enough with this sort of thing, these random career experiments, to know that the minute I lost my enthusiasm would be the minute the whole gig turned sour.

While two paramedics loitered nearby, I pulled the suit over my head, stuck my arms through the armholes, and found the spot for my face to go through. Chris yanked the bottom hem down, but something about the outfit's symmetry was a little off. The big jutting tip of the banana coming out of my head was a bit top heavy. I realized that to get my face to stick out of the middle, I had to jut my neck forward and balance the weight so that the tip didn't flop forward. This threw off my center of gravity, which I could only regain by spreading my legs hip distance apart and bending my knees at about a 45-degree angle. It wasn't attractive (although I kept the faith by imagining that I could probably find someone on the Internet, in a matter of seconds, who would think so). Chris piled a few bunches of bananas into my arms, and I hurtled out into the open space.

The minute I stepped out into the plaza, some kid yelled "Hey! It's a banana!" and four or five others came charging at me. Adrenaline surged through my body as I greeted them head on. My only instructions were: Pass out all the bananas, have a good time, and occasionally insert the name of the company into my exchanges with the general public (e.g., "Free bananas from The Fruit Guys!" or "Stay healthy with The Fruit Guys!"). I handed each kid a banana, which went smoothly enough, but when I tried to sloganeer, an unfamiliar voice came out: "Enjoy your delicious bananas! Courtesy of The Fruit Guys!" I sounded like a Top 40 deejay. "Bananas! Brought to you by The Fruit Guys!" Why couldn't I talk in my normal voice? I'd suddenly become one of Phil Hartman's characters on *The Simpsons*. Of course, I knew exactly what was happening. As a natural defense mechanism, I was adopting an ironic way of speaking to let myself know that I was in on my own joke. My God, living in the modern world puts a lot of strain on the unconscious mind.

There wasn't a lot I could do in the costume, physically speaking. (Mentally, of course, I was stretching all sorts of muscles.) For the first twenty-five minutes, it was all I could do to just peel off a new banana fast enough to satisfy the cluster of people mobbing me. More than once, when faced with a delay in my delivery system, someone blurted out, "Just hand me the whole bunch. I'll do it myself!" Everything had seemed so mellow when I'd first shown up at the plaza a few minutes earlier, but now that The Fruit Guys' Banana was on the scene—not to brag—it seemed to give the whole event a nucleus. Most of the other freebies that day were of the discount coupon and blood pressure testing variety. There might have been free key chains in the mix, but I was the only one giving away something with a retail value of more than fifteen cents. *This must be what it feels like to be armed with a stash of single Kool Menthols in the prison yard*, I thought.

With all the attention on me, I knew that whenever I had a chance, I should try to do something to make myself visually interesting, even if it just meant running a wind sprint back to the booth when I replenished my supply. If there was anyone like me in the crowd, their whole day could easily be made by watching a banana charge at top speed across a large urban plaza at high noon. Or maybe, to get totally *meta*, I could stage a pratfall where I slipped on a banana peel.

Halfway into my shift, the initial excitement wore off, and I started to drag a little. It was exceptionally hot outside, and the suit had become somewhat of a Dutch oven, first reaching a critical heat and then sealing in the juices. Soon enough, everyone stopped receiving a free smile with their banana. And then, over by a booth whose only attribute seemed to be a large plastic replica of an artery, I saw a group of kids crowding around and screaming excitedly. When they parted, a towering, royal blue muscleman with a yellow lightning bolt affixed to his head came backflipping in my direction.

"Who's that?" I asked the woman who was currently hugging me.

"That's Thunder, Banana Lady!" A lot of people, without prompting, were automatically calling me Banana Lady, which I liked. "You've never seen Thunder?"

I opened my mouth, and my cheesy radio deejay voice said, "No, I've never seen Thunder!"

Thunder, it turned out, was the mascot for the Golden State Warriors and one heck of a gymnast. He finished off his series of handsprings with a perfect backflip and turned around to face me. I tried to get down on my knees to pay him homage, but the lower curve of the banana got in the way and was folding up into my chin as I attempted to get my feet tucked underneath me. Luckily, the hugging woman came to the rescue by grabbing my arm and pulling me toward Thunder, who had both of his oversized, foam-muscled arms raised in the air. I couldn't help but notice his suit was in perfect condition. It fit him like a spandex glove.

"Dance!" the lady commanded, slapping her ass a few times. "Brick House" was blasting out of the speakers, and a few spirited office-working souls decided to join her, security laminates swinging around their necks. It was getting crazy out here, coworkers getting all funky with one another like they were one leg in a blackout at the office Christmas party. Thunder took my hands, and I wondered for a moment what this was going to lead to. I imagined a full-on, dirty dancing, free-for-all starring Banana Lady and Thunder. Maybe someone would take a picture of us for one of those fun featurettes they do on slow news days, and we'd forever be linked in the public's imagination. Instead, he swung me around a few times, my curves regrettably enforcing an arm's distance between us, and then ended with a suave plié followed by that move where you bow and then roll one hand down in front of you in a courtly manner. I was flattered, but I wasn't going to kid myself. I'm sure he paid special attention to all the mascots he encountered, danced with any piece of costumed fruit that appeared at the same event as he did. Even if things with Thunder didn't go any further, I could appreciate finally meeting an icon who fully understood the scope his job. He knew he was supposed to be the life of the party and didn't back down for a second. I had a lot to learn.

Finally, a man in a bright orange vest announced through a megaphone that the big event, the 5-K walk/run to celebrate the cardiovascular system, was starting. Thunder bounded over to the starting line, spinning around mid-leap to motion for me to follow him. I started to run but was foiled by The Fruit Guys, who told me we were out of free bananas to pass out, and I was officially off duty.

"Well, maybe I should just go and do the run anyway?" I said to Chris, even though I was severely overheated, wearing large black boots, and already winded from dancing.

"You really don't have to," he said, handing me forty-five bucks.

I stood on my toes and saw Thunder encircled by a group of kids. I decided the dignified thing to do was to just leave, to set him free so he could keep on flip-flopping his way into everyone's hearts.

I knew he wasn't looking over at me, but I waved anyway, noticing it wasn't a jokey, theatrical wave, but my actual, real wave. Then I bent over, put my arms over my head, and let Chris pull the suit off me in a giant sucking motion. I pocketed my money and went home to my husband, our son, and a new pack of tube socks.

12
SKIPPIN' OVER THE OCEAN LIKE A STONE

When Eli and I visit my parents, we can be reasonably sure what's going to transpire over the course of a few hours. More often than not, barbecue sauce is involved. Usually there's some kind of televised sporting event happening in the background—"sport" being a loose term that includes any contest combining discipline and raw human emotion. The Westminster Dog Show or Celebrity Poker qualify. When the clock in the kitchen appears to be safely past 5:00 P.M. (by at least three or four minutes), my dad declares that "Attitude Adjustment Hour" has arrived and begins whipping up cocktails for everyone. Well, everyone except for my brother Paul who drinks *a lot* of Coke and unwinds by reading *TV Guide* from cover to cover each week. Paul, who lives with my parents and is therefore relieved of any duty to socialize, usually limits his commentary to reviewing the meal with his trademark rating system:

"That was good."

"That was good. I liked it."

"That was good. I liked it. Let's have it again sometime."

"That was good. I liked it. I think I'll have seconds." (Rare)

At the end of the night, my mom puts on a big pot of decaf and throws fourteen leftover ribs, five ears of corn, a dozen biscuits, a pint of three-bean salad, four rolls of toilet paper, a can opener, and a stack of manila envelopes in a grocery bag, and we drive home.

Visiting Eli's family bears only the slightest resemblance to visiting mine—in that they also live in a house with a roof on top of it. The first time we flew to Tucson after Gus was born, Eli's mom, Penny, had gotten caught up at an event and dispatched Eli's stepdad, Gordon, to pick us up.

"Penny says that if you want to come down and meet them at the festival, we could get some dinner after that," Gordon told us.

"Them? Who's them?" Eli asked, giving me the eye.

Gordon's voice went a little lovey-dovey: "I'm sure she told you about Carolyn."

Right. Carolyn. Was she the retired parole officer or the fat activist? Maybe the school counselor/mountain climber? In the five years that I'd known Eli, his mother had had a number of different girlfriends, but it was hard to keep them straight because she always seemed to be "taking a break" from one, giving another "some space," or deciding if she wanted to commit to being "the secondary partner in a polyamorous triad."

"Maybe we should go to the fair," I said, leaning forward so Gordon could hear me over our son Gus, who started complaining the second we strapped him into his car seat. "The little dude might be into it after sitting on that plane for three hours."

Having recently become a parent, I found that things like fairs had taken on new appeal. I didn't care what kind of fair it was or what it featured. Whether there were pie-eating contests and animal slaughter, smooth jazz and overpriced crafts, faulty tilt-a-whirls and carnies with Hep C, anything that would tire Gus out and make him sleep more than two-and-a-half hours in a row sounded better than being trapped in the house while he ate a box of Kleenex or repeatedly shimmied up a floor lamp.

"Yeah . . ." Gordon said, "um, actually, probably not." He glanced in the rearview mirror and changed lanes. "They're at something called the Sex Workers Art Festival."

God, I should have known! Penny is one of those ladies you find at every cultural event taking place in her community, wearing a brightly colored vest; large, unusual jewelry; and a pair of comfortable sandals. She always knows when the Senegalese National Ballet is coming to town and is on a first-name basis with every fabric artist in the county. The weekend we were visiting, we learned, her schedule had been completely taken over by the Sex Workers. She even skipped her weekly gay square dancing night because she was too busy going to workshops, panels, and performances. How could she miss the two-hour long "Sacred Prostitute" lecture that explored "spiritual sexuality in therapeutic practice?" And what about the workshop on "breath orgasm" and the BDSM seminar on the fine art of flogging that promised to end the weekend "with both a bang and a whimper?"

It's not that I didn't want Gus to go—he had long been cracking up at the sight of ass cheeks hanging out of a pair of chaps. I had just hoped that being in Tucson would actually mean a vacation from the constant throbbing of performative sexuality that hovers over San Francisco like the fog itself. Was it now impossible to go anywhere without being encouraged to view my cervix or witness a parade of female ejaculators? Did anybody alive hear the word "harness" and still think of horses? When did we all become a bunch of whores? These were the sort of questions I was asking myself, until Gordon handed me a newspaper feature on the event, and I realized that I knew half the people in the photo.

"Let's skip it," I said. "I don't need any more free lube."

When Penny and Carolyn arrived home, Penny was glowing from the experience. Partly, she just loves to learn new things and interact with new people. She loves "to dialogue" about "issues" in her "community." I think she also really enjoys being a little wild—being the sixty-year-old lady who takes everything in stride, who can never be shocked, or the rare Jewish mom who never gets verklempt.

While Penny whipped up a batch of kale and corn squares, Carolyn approached me in the living room. At first glance, Carolyn looked exactly like someone who immediately gets pegged as a lesbian by people who hadn't met too many lesbians: broad shoulders, no makeup, close-cropped hair (the gym teacher type. This also describes a few of my straight Midwestern relatives). She may have been six-feet tall, with the ruddy tan of a true outdoorswoman who was still kayaking in Central America and climbing mountains in Nepal as she entered her seventies, but inside she was just a sweet, genteel Southern belle.

"Yew know, Bayeth," she said. Her voice was surprisingly soft and delicate. "Ah'm jist naht showa 'bout this wirkshawp Pinny and ah wint to. Ah wanted to enjoy mahsayelf, but ah found it a little awhd."

"Oh, it was just incredible," Penny called in from the kitchen. "The fisting workshop!"

Eli was playing with Gus out on the back patio. "Eli!" I yelled. "Did you hear why your mom couldn't pick us up from the airport?"

"Yeah, yeah," he said, "I know, The Sex Workers."

"Well, yeah," I said. "They were teaching her how to properly insert her fist into a lady's vagina!"

Penny came in drying her hands on a towel, hands that suddenly looked different to me. "Oh, it was fantastic!" she said. "Okay, it's time to eat, everybody!"

Eli brought Gus in and got him situated in his high chair.

"They did one demonstration with a woman volunteer from the audience," Penny continued. "And then, they got a guy up there!"

"They did a *guy?*" Gordon piped in, suddenly interested. "You didn't tell me they were going to do a guy!"

"Hey, hey, hey!" Eli said, bringing his index finger sharply across his throat over and over again. "I don't want to hear about anybody's fists while I'm eating my dinner, okay? I'm glad there's a movement to empower all you gay senior citizens about your sexuality or whatever, but Jesus."

After dinner, I got Carolyn alone in the kitchen. I had only known her a short while but had already grown very fond of her. This household needed someone with her sense of decorum, and I wanted to make sure she stuck around for awhile.

"Listen to me, Carolyn," I said with an obvious sense of urgency. "I think it's really admirable that you're open to exploring these things, but—"

"Ah know. Ah'm jist tryin' to, you know, broaden mah horizons for Pinny."

"Right, right," I said. "That's sweet of you, but listen to me now. There is no reason on earth that you shouldn't think it's weird to go to a fisting workshop."

"Yeah?" She seemed relieved to be hearing this from someone.

"It's fine for some people, to each his own, blah, blah, different strokes, all that," I said, peering into the living room to make sure nobody was listening. "But it's not, like, a normal thing to do. If it makes you feel strange to see a woman sprawled out on a table in a public space impaled upon a latex-covered human arm, that's perfectly reasonable. Remember that. Just don't let Penny tell you

194

you're somehow too conservative or emotionally shut down because you find that strange."

She hugged me, and I felt some tension leaving her enormous shoulders.

The next night one of Penny and Gordon's closest friends came over to the house. I had heard them speak about Greta before in reverent tones. She was a therapist who had coauthored a best-selling book with one of her clients, a successful businessman who was continually confronted with psychic evidence that he had been St. Paul in a past life. Greta had done past life regression on Penny and Gordon numerous times before, and we had heard the results: Penny had once traversed the Gobi desert alone, on foot, to watch a child being born. Gordon had been a Native American boy who was mauled by a bear, a cloistered Chinese monk, and a small animal squashed by a giant foot shortly after his birth. He once went through an entire session speaking in an Irish brogue.

I immediately sensed that if anyone could guide a person to speak with the angels teeming inside, it was Greta. A statuesque woman with a silvery shock of hair, sparkly eyes, and a warm smile, all she needed to portray an angel on a modern TV series was an ivory cashmere pullover and some attractive, cream-colored, woolen slacks.

I asked her a lot of questions about her work, including one that must be at the top of the FAQ list for hypnotists: "What if you're too jaded and cynical and cautious to ever let anyone else be in control?" Pouring another shot of liquid amino acids on her casserole, Penny encouraged me to try it out. "Just think of it as a drug trip."

"Not really being a drug person, Penny," I said, "that might not be the right strategy for me."

At that, she slammed her open palm down on the table. "How did I end up with such straight kids?" she laughed, looking over at Eli. "Straight kids who are in a monogamous relationship even!" And then she paused. "You guys are monogamous, right? I'm just assuming because you're married, but I don't want to jump to conclusions because, of course, we're all aware that there are many different models for making a relationship work, and if you are open-minded and able to communicate effectively, then you can. . . ."

The next morning after breakfast, as Penny was pouring her homemade granola into an earthenware bowl after doing isolation exercises for her sciatica, she and Gordon gave me a surprise birthday present: a free past life regression therapy session with Greta, scheduled for that afternoon.

"You seemed so interested," they explained. "We thought you'd like to try it out for yourself!"

I was quite surprised, as my presents from them had been previously limited to fun scarves and Ziploc bags of their homemade granola, which, it should be pointed out, is a recipe that has been perfected over forty years. The best granola ever—I was comfortable with that. But sending a friend to go spelunking into my psyche?

After some hemming and hawing, they convinced me that it was going to be really fun, and all I had to do was be *myselves*.

They dropped me off at her office and wished me luck. I stood there in the middle of the strip mall parking lot, the warm winter sun beaming onto my face, watching the car peel out and feeling increasingly nervous. I was back to the FAQ: How could I let a complete stranger hypnotize me? I was a pretty good liar, so maybe I could just fake it. While Greta tried to put me under, I could distract myself with muffin recipes or TV theme songs until she thought I was under the spell, and then—drawing from what I'd learned about Penny's and Gordon's sessions—just start babbling about exotic landscapes mixed in with some birth and death.

Greta welcomed me into her cozy office, and I immediately felt like curling up in her comfy leather chair for a nap. My ironic detachment also felt like taking a nap, which seemed like bad timing. I just knew that, within five minutes, I would be licking my paws like a cat. God, I hoped I wasn't a cat in a former life. Or what if the hypnosis acted as some form of truth serum, and I just starting purging my soul of all the terrible and embarrassing things I had done in this life? What if something in my brain slipped around, and I started admitting to things I'd never actually done? I envisioned myself explaining to Greta in great detail how to dismember a body or methodically laying out the best strategies for luring a child into your conversion van.

I settled down and began to breathe deeply to calm myself.

Was she piping something through the ventilation system that was making me melt into this chair? Wow, look at all those teeny, tiny holes in the ceiling! What if inside each and every one of those teeny, tiny holes was an entire teeny, tiny universe in which little past life regression therapists were hypnotizing little confused mom characters. I wonder if their voices would sound like Chipmunky cartoon voices. . . . Just when I was about to nod off, Greta said that, before we began visiting my former selves, I should come up with an issue I was dealing with in this lifetime to focus on during the regression. Was there anything I wanted to work on? Problems? Blockages?

Naturally, even in my semiconscious state, I didn't want to go too deep. I'm a firm believer in the method of maintaining an even keel by ignoring whatever may be lurking underneath the surface— if, in fact, there is anything under the surface. I yawned and tried to think of something tangentially related to my life, but nothing that would leave me out there raw and exposed. Was there an issue involving curbside recycling or desktop preferences for my computer? Maybe something a little more revealing, like how whenever I splurged on an expensive beauty product, say, a shampoo or moisturizer, I could never bring myself to completely finish up the bottle. I would buy a new, cheap shampoo and start using that, but still hang on to the expensive one, even if there was barely any left. My bathroom cabinet was full of near empty bottles of products that rich people buy. Maybe that was a deep enough issue. But Greta had a strange hold on me: I was already being honest with her when I didn't want to be.

"Well, I have sort of a problem with my 'career.'" I made the air quotes with my fingers, which really said it all.

"Okay, go on. . . ."

"I have no problem writing stuff or doing shows, but when it comes to 'taking it to the next level'"—again with the air quotes—"I constantly sabotage myself. I would love to make money doing what I love and not have to worry about getting a job in an office again, but I'm having a problem taking myself seriously because what I do seems sort of frivolous."

Greta dimmed the lights and walked back to her chair. I can't believe I was about to go under and find out why I was unable to shoot for the stars. I felt like a raging egomaniac. Hello, I'm here to find out what is stopping me from reaching my true potential. Even an idiot would know that what I really needed was a trip to the scientology center.

She put a cassette into a recorder, turned it on, and told me to place it on the table next to me. Now the tape was running, recording the entire session for posterity, blackmail, or comedic exploitation.

"Beth, I want you to close your eyes and relax. Acknowledge the thoughts that cross your mind, and let them move on. We're going to go into a deeply relaxed state. . . . Now I want you to picture a cave. It can be any kind of cave you want—natural or man-made."

Man-made? I hadn't begun to picture anything, but when she said that, I instantly flashed on an image of a small papier-mâché cave, like one in a diorama, which I could pick up and move if I needed to.

GRETA: Walk inside your cave and feel yourself in the darkness. Now when I count to three you'll step out the other side. One . . . two . . . three. Where are you?

ME: I'm standing in a jungle. It's very hot and sunny out, but there's a lot of shade underneath these huge green trees. There are vines everywhere, and I almost feel like . . . I almost feel like I'm an animal. [*Laughing*] Well, maybe not. Can I . . . ?

GRETA: It's okay. You can be an animal. Are you an animal?

ME: I think I'm a monkey. Some kind of South American monkey.

GRETA: Hey! That sounds fun!

ME: Yeah, it feels pretty fun so far. I'm waiting for somebody. I'm in a tree, and I'm waiting to see somebody down below. It feels like it's a joke, a trick. I'm not going to hurt anybody, but I'm going to jump down there and surprise them when they walk past."

[*Long pause*]

GRETA: Have they shown up yet? Do you see them?

ME: No, not yet. I'm still waiting in the tree.

[*Long pause*]

200

GRETA: Anything?

ME: No. . . . Oh, wait. I see him. It's an explorer.

GRETA: How do you know he's an explorer?

ME: Well, he's dressed up like a safari guy. He has on khaki shorts and sort of a pith helmet and one of those shirts with those things on the shoulders.

GRETA: Epaulets.

ME: Yeah, epaulets. And whatever kind of monkey I am, I'm going to screw up his research when he sees me. My kind of monkey is not supposed to be in this jungle.

GRETA: So what do you do?

ME: I jump down on him.

GRETA: And what happens?

ME: He thinks it's funny, and we become friends. I jump on his shoulder, and he takes me out of the jungle and onto a boat.

GRETA: What's going on with your forehead?

[At this point, my forehead has launched into a series of spasms that I can't control. It feels like there are marionette strings attached to the muscles in my forehead with fish hooks, and they are being controlled by three or four epileptics. It is totally involuntary, and I can tell it must look really weird.]

ME: Uh, I don't know. I can't help it.

GRETA: Okay.

ME: I think it's helping me somehow.

GRETA: Okay. Let's move on to the next significant event in this monkey's life. One . . . two . . . three.

ME: I see a man with a top hat and a tuxedo and a cane—kind of twenties era. Pinstripe pants, a handlebar mustache. He's doing a show in a dinner theater, and I'm sitting at a table with candles watching the show. I have wavy, brown hair, and I'm wearing a red dress, like a flapper. I'm sitting by myself at the table, and I think I'm going to sleep with him after the show is done.

GRETA: Wait. Are you still the monkey?

ME: No. I'm a lady. Is that okay?

GRETA: Yes, that's perfectly fine. As you watch the show, what is your reaction to his performance?

ME: I'm really enthralled with him. There's an orchestra, and he's dancing. People are enjoying the show, though I'm annoyed that they are so subdued. He's kind of goofy. It looks like a comedy dance routine. Like he falls down and then a big brass horn honks. Braaap!

GRETA: What happens next?

ME: The show is over, and he comes and sits down next to me. He's suave and older than me. He's trying to charm me. We're definitely not married, and I'm kind of suspicious of him. I think he's married already. I should be on guard, but I'm attracted to him. We talk, and it feels very exciting, but I decide to leave. Even though I'm flattered by his attention, I don't want to be another notch on his belt. I act like I'm a little more shy than I really am, so he doesn't think that it's his fault that I'm leaving.

GRETA: Interesting.

ME: I'm also not from this town. Nobody else knows where I am. I came a long way to see him; I got all dressed up, but I'm going back to my hotel now. I leave the club and walk alone in the dark up a hill. I feel very safe and happy with my decision. But when I get to the hotel, I immediately ask the front desk clerk to call the club and get the performer on the phone because I've changed my mind. I've decided that I actually do want to sleep with him. I wait while they try to find him, but he's already left, I'm sure with some other lady. I go back up to the room, and I get in bed, and it takes me a long time to fall asleep.

GRETA: Let's move forward again to the next significant event.

ME: I see Texas—like the outline of the state, like it is on a map. A ranch and a tractor.

GRETA: Are we leaving that woman behind?

ME: I guess so because this feels very bright and more open. Less clandestine. There are wheat fields. It's almost like a painting. The sky is very blue. It's flat and boring, and I'm looking down on it from the sky. I see a house and kids running around outside the house. Ugh. Four or five kids. And I'm a housewife. I have that hair that's parted down the middle and pulled back in a severe bun, a long dress with an apron over it. I'm holding a pot, but I'm standing out-side. The kids are all running around pulling on my skirt. I'm ex-hausted. I'm feeling trapped. I'm looking up at the sky, wondering how I'm ever going to get out of there. My husband is out in the field, but I have no connection to him at all. He's out there doing the work, and he comes back and eats dinner.

203

GRETA: Okay, now slow down. Try to stretch forward ten or twenty years. Where is she now?

ME: Hey, her husband is dead! She and her sister are living together, and she's seeing things in a new way. I have no idea where the kids are. She feels very out of it. All these things have passed her by. There are inventions that she hasn't heard of. They're walking down the street, and her sister is telling her something about the social and political climate in the country. Her sister is kind of bringing her around and teaching her a lot. And she feels shy and is kind of embarrassed, like a dumb hick. How is she ever going to keep up? She feels this loss of experience.

GRETA: You may want to look toward her death.

[Long silence as I picture the woman sweating profusely in bed as her sister mops her brow with a damp cloth.]

GRETA: Okay, let's go back to the tunnel. Turning toward the exit. Looking for the next story. One . . . two . . . three, and out.

ME: It feels kind of like the early sixties. Everything's very brightly colored, like a beach town. I'm a ten-year-old boy on a skateboard. I'm wearing a blue shirt and tan shorts and no shoes, and I'm skateboarding down this Southern California street. Everybody in the neighborhood really likes me a lot, and I'm really friendly to all the adults. I go to the beach where my older brother is surfing. Then we go to a hamburger stand.

GRETA: Move forward to what happens next.

ME: I'm really good in high school, and when I graduate, I go some-where to take pictures. I'm a photographer. I'm in Cambodia taking pictures, but it's not war. I'm documenting these people in their vil-lages, and they take me in, and I live there for awhile. I'm by myself, but I don't feel alone. I don't want the government to know that I'm there. I'm hiding out with them and avoiding the war. I'm going back to my hometown, but it feels different, and I wish I was a kid again. I was at my best when I was the kid on the skateboard. I go to a neighborhood bar, and everyone feels sorry for me because I'm kind of a sad sack. I never want anything to change.

GRETA: And back to the tunnel. Once again, heading out. One . . . two . . . three.

ME: I see gloomy train tracks in the rain. I'm walking along the tracks in a yellow raincoat. I have a big hat on. I'm kind of tough.

GRETA: Are you a man or a woman?

ME: A woman, sort of a butch woman. I'm doing some kind of job. I'm supposed to be checking for something as I'm walking down the tracks. There's a river next to me, and I see a lodge of some sort. I have to go to different crossings and write things down. A lot of other women wouldn't have this job. I go back to where I live. I live by myself. I'm making dinner, a big stew. I'm waiting for someone to call me with good news.

GRETA: The phone rings. Pick it up.

ME: It's my mother. Somebody had a baby, and I'm really excited for them, even though I'm not sure if I'll ever go and visit my fam-ily. I like the isolation too much. I like being by myself in my cabin.

It's not that I hate people, I just don't want to be around them very often.

GRETA: Okay. Is there anything else this woman needs to tell you?

ME: I don't think so. Just that it's okay to live in the woods by yourself and be happy.

GRETA: Okay. When I count to three, you will go back inside the cave, and when you come out, you will be here. One . . . two . . . three.

[*End tape transcription*]

I opened my eyes, feeling extremely relaxed. I remembered everything that happened and was somehow not embarrassed by the fact that I had just spent nearly an hour speaking aloud my stream of consciousness. As a matter of fact, I was kind of proud of myself for coming up with all those characters. The farmer's wife! The photographer in Cambodia during the Vietnam War! Surely that was pretty good stuff. As Greta smiled at me, I was certain she was marveling at how fascinating and unique my past lives were compared to some of her other clients. I didn't have to be a Carthaginian princess or a medieval inquisitor. My "everyday people" approach gave me a lot more credibility. Very Studs Terkel, I thought. Just as I was debating whether I should spring for another session to uncover whatever other intriguing souls happened to be occupying my psyche, Greta pulled the tape out of the recorder and said, "I'm going to give this tape an appropriate title." She took out her pen, wrote something down, and handed it to me. In all caps it read "VALIDATION."

And I did feel somewhat validated by this process. Everyone seems to place a lot of value on having an "old soul," and now it looked like I could join the club. Although I was perfectly prepared to stick around awhile and analyze what we'd just been through together, Greta looked as though she might have another appointment. Getting up to show me out, she said, "It's so refreshing to regress someone who doesn't need therapy at all." Then the door quietly clicked shut.

Still a little dazed, I walked outside to wait for my ride. I wondered what she'd meant by that, about me not needing therapy. Am I that normal? Were the lives that I'd just conjured completely run-of-the-mill examples of scenarios that everybody has? Maybe getting VALIDATION written on your tape is like getting a pat on the head. *Nice job. Thanks for trying to play with us. Move along. We introspective types don't need your kind around here.* But how could that be? That last lady, my isolated cabin dweller, seemed like kind of an interesting character, somewhat mysterious, living alone in the Pacific Northwest. As I reenvisioned her story, I noticed that the train tracks with the river next to them seemed vaguely familiar, until I realized the railroad worker heavily resembled the Log Lady from the television series *Twin Peaks*. Oh, no. I cribbed my past life from a television show? Did I not have an original thought in my head? I started panicking as I flipped through my other lives.

What about the Southern California skateboarder before that?

The way I first pictured him . . . No! It was nearly a play-by-play replication of the first scene of that movie, what was it called? Oh, Lord. *Almost Famous*. "Almost?" "Famous?" Get it? That whole thing I had revealed to her about not having a career? If I were any more obvious, I would have rabbit ears and a remote control.

And what about my rural housewife? The woman in the vast wheat field looking at the old farmhouse? It dawned on me that I'd appropriated the *exact* image from that famous Andrew Wyeth painting. I tried to cheer up by congratulating myself on at least incorporating another medium. Painting is deeper than TV, right? Then I realized that the rest of that scenario was straight out of *Little House on the Prairie*. It was hopeless. The dancing man with the handlebar mustache? Exactly like a comedy sketch on an old episode of *Mr. Show* with David Cross and Bob Odenkirk, both of whom I would probably sleep with if I were ever drunk in New Orleans.

To add to the humiliation, you might notice that I was strictly moving around the border states of the country I currently lived in. In a clockwise fashion even! If you'd given me another hour, I would have found myself in Montana, Minnesota, Maryland, and Florida. And not only was I a bunch of Americans, but also I remained exclusively in the twentieth century the whole time.

Thank God, at least I still had my monkey. Yes, I was born in the year of the monkey, and my first book was called *Monkey Girl*, so there was some connection with this monkey who . . . likes tricks and jumps onto the shoulder of an explorer who's walking through the jungle and takes him back to his house by boat. Why, of course. Curious George. I'd just been reading it to Gus the night before.

I sat down on the curb, a little dejected, trying not to be depressed. I imagined a future version of me regressing to this version of me, reporting from some space-time continuum far, far away and looking onto this scene: a lonely mom under a palm tree in an empty parking lot in the desert clutching a cassette tape that says VALIDATION. *This probably looks pretty good to an outsider*, I told myself. *This probably looks pretty deep.*

13

LITTLE BUNDLE OF ENTROPY

A few months after my son was born, a woman named Cheryl phoned me and said she had a "baby-warming" gift for us. This struck me as slightly weird, as she was a waitress at a restaurant I used to frequent, not someone I knew very well. I was discovering that this is what happens when you have a baby. Certain people gladly take the opportunity to duck out of your life forever, but they're quickly replaced by other people: The Baby People. Personally, I was never into babies, especially right after having one, but I was finding it difficult to duck out of my own life. Out of necessity, I declared that my mission would be to embrace The Baby People, learn their customs, and pray that some of their enthusiasm rubbed off on me.

My cheery new friend Cheryl's gift wasn't fuzzy or flame-retardant, and it didn't squeak or have ears sewn on it. Not that I was expecting anything traditional, but even I was taken aback when she asked, "Would you like to come over, so that I can teach you how to massage your baby?"

I swallowed hard and tried to remember how I usually responded to questions I've never been asked before—or, for that matter, questions that I never even knew existed. I usually said yes. I also considered my hips and thighs, which had recently undergone some expansion, and figured I might as well crank open my mind a little more, too.

I'd never heard of a baby massage, but I was also the sort of person who, prior to giving birth, had changed exactly one diaper in her entire life. And I did it wrong. This could have been the most common activity in the world, as popular as all the other phenomena I never knew about—like Boppies, BabyBjörn, Ultrasaucers, and Whoozits—and I was simply too out of the loop to know. And a big part of me was excited by the prospect of something new to do with Gus. Let's face it, there's not a whole lot you can do with someone who has only been alive for three months. By 7:30 every morning, after a boob fest and a little dancing, I was usually fresh out of ideas.

"Is it dangerous?" I asked Cheryl. "It sounds like if you do it wrong, you could smash some underdeveloped organ or jostle an important neurotransmitter." I desperately wanted it to be dangerous. After dangling soft toys in front of Gus's face while he lolled around in the pastel Tender Vibes chair, I was craving something a little risky. I hadn't even had to put a Band-Aid on him yet. Bathtub peekaboo, when I took both my hands off of his slippery little body for a second until he started to list perilously toward the water, had lost its edge weeks ago. I was starting to miss the good old days of drunk driving and casual sex.

"Yes, Cheryl," I said. "I would love to bring my baby over to your house, so you can show me how to massage it."

"Um, it's a him, right?" she asked, obviously a little taken aback that I would refer to my child as an inanimate object—a habit I was finding hard to break.

"Yes! Him!" I corrected. "So I can learn how to massage *him*."

I hung up the phone feeling pretty good. Saying yes to Cheryl went along nicely with my whole plan to play this mom thing by ear. Things would suddenly come up, and I would think on my feet, like an early American settler or game show contestant. I was convinced that if millions of people could parent poorly and feel inadequate in the process, so could I. Or maybe the problem was that everyone was just doing too much research. In times of self-doubt, I have always found it reassuring to think of being *too* informed as a tragic flaw. I would feel it out, just as I'd previously approached shooting pool and ice skating—two things I knew I would never master, but wasn't too embarrassed to do in public. The one and only ground rule I had going into motherhood was a refusal to dress Gus in ironic heavy metal shirts or give him temporary tattoos. To me, that was as upsetting as putting sunglasses on your dog.

The morning of the first baby massage session, I decided to stop and get Cheryl some flowers on the way. I had heard so many people complain about self-absorbed new moms that I thought this would give me a leg up. "Look how I care about you!" my Gerber daisies would announce defensively on my behalf. It sounds sick, but I really believed this. The daisies were totally worth the nine dollars.

So I pulled Gus out of the car and walked up to a sidewalk flower shop. As I was looking around, an old coworker passed by and did a double take.

"Hey! I thought that was you!" she said. "Wow, I had no idea!"

"What?" I said, shaking my head.

"That you were even pregnant! Look at your baby!"

Yeah, look at him. Wow was right. I was so used to having him around me every second of the day, drooling into my neck, reaching into my mouth, coiled into my boobs like a gastropod, that I hadn't stopped to think about how others saw him. He was like my elbows or my sofa. Unfortunately, when I brought him out of the house this morning, I hadn't realized how truly terrible he looked.

My excuse for everything that went wrong during that particular month—from the Tequila Incident to the Garbage Can Fiasco—was that Eli was on a five-week national tour with one of his bands. I couldn't resent the fact that he had ditched us for rock and roll because I would have done the same thing. To be honest, I was kicking myself for not getting my shit together during my first trimester to learn to play an instrument, form a new band, make a record, print up some T-shirts, and book a tour that began a few weeks after giving birth. How I compensated, and learned to feel worse in the process, was by constantly watching a split screen in my head that contrasted Eli's activities with my own.

There's Eli affixing a sticker to his bass case from some cool new band he just met backstage. There I am affixing a deodorizer to the side of the rancid diaper pail I just hosed out in the backyard. There's Eli eating barbecue in Nashville on a sunny spring afternoon. There I am eating burned cheese off the oven rack on a dark, foggy morning. There's Eli, glistening with sweat, chatting up a cute indie rock girl after the show. There I am, covered in vomit, barking out orders to the indifferent diaper service man after a crying jag. It was a time in my life when "keeping it together" meant trying really hard to make it past noon without curling up in the fetal position on the living room rug. I was very tired. Consequently, I was experiencing the emotional and personal hygiene challenges associated with sleep deprivation—and/or mental illness. And Gus didn't appear to be in much better shape.

"So, how old is she?" the old coworker said, craning her neck to inspect him.

"Oh, he's a he," I said. "Gus."

"Oh my God," she said. "I am *so* sorry. Just with the outfit, I thought . . ."

Jesus Christ. Look what I had him wearing.

The three people we knew who had kids were funneling clothes to us via an endless stream of grocery bags that ended up in the closet. I hadn't been interfacing too much with the washing machine, so when Gus needed a change of clothes, I would throw the dirty outfit onto the back porch, shut the door, and dig something else out of one of the grocery bags. Grateful as I was, some of the stuff we received was gnarly, if only because nobody had ever bothered to filter out the stock. The bags just kept getting passed down from family to family, as if it were bad luck to incinerate a nubby, formula-covered terry cloth sleeper that your baby had once pooped in while grabbing your finger for the first time. Just looking at those items was like getting an instant injection of someone else's sleepless night or queasy stomach. I saw them as carriers of mild misery, undesirable and possibly contagious. Yet still, when the cream of the crop had risen and spoiled, I would return to the bags in the closet like a monkey to the shit pile, digging for the lesser of evils.

"Well, that's cool," the lady said and then started in on some cheerleading about how powerful it was that I was screwing the binary gender assignment roles, as if I had purposefully devised the best way to make my baby succeed as a progressive social statement. She continued on about blue and pink and trucks and Barbies, how all the world's children were subjected to inherent sexism. Boys need to cry, too! Girls don't really want to be princesses! Zzzzzzzzzz. I don't know. I had trouble listening because I was far more riveted by my child's appearance.

This was my son, right here in my arms. He was dressed in a hideous pale yellow zippered jumpsuit that was covered with big pink umbrellas shielding little pink mice from fat pink raindrops. It was about two sizes too big, so I'd rolled up the sleeves and legs in a way that made Gus look like he was anchored by four doughnuts. His Peter Pan collar was frayed and curled at the edges. The entire front of his outfit was splattered with cherry red stains of Children's Tylenol, gummy enough to have picked up dirt and food scraps from my kitchen floor. My baby was wearing onion skins.

But it wasn't just his clothes. Gus had dried milk around the corners of his mouth, and there were yellow flakes of cradle cap on his head, which I had given up trying to comb out weeks ago because I couldn't take the screaming. Some website said it would eventually fall out on its own, and I chose to believe that. Thankfully, his baby acne had mostly disappeared, except for intense eruptions on each of his cheeks that made him look like he'd been dusted with theatrical rouge ground from pebbles. His tiny microfleece booties, a gift from someone who'd been convinced we were having a girl, were hot pink. He was not a pretty sight, and to make matters worse, neither was I. We should have been on a bus shelter advertisement for birth control.

I grabbed my flowers and made a quick exit, disgruntled by how everyone who passed seemed to be silently judging us. I hadn't realized that Gus, by virtue of not being able to talk or think too deeply yet, had basically become my new accessory. He was like a burbling, drooling handbag or a warm, sticky scarf that could breathe. Months into the game, I had finally learned the valuable lesson of why people try really hard to make babies look cute: (1) They are perfect for deflecting attention away from yourself. (2) If they look good, they can make you look better. (3) A mom with a dirty, disheveled baby looks like a crazy person.

On my way back to the car, I heard someone calling my name. I hurried my pace and pretended not to hear, acting like it had just dawned on me to urgently communicate with Gus.

"Look at these pretty flowers, little dude!! This one is *pink*!! This color is called *o-range*!!" I was yelling to drown out the guy's voice, but trying to juggle the baby, the flowers, and my car keys proved to be too much. I eventually got busted while getting Gus into the car seat.

"Hey, mama!"

Everyone really likes to call you "mama" when you first have a baby.

He was a musician in a local band who knew me and Eli. He had seen me a number of times while I was pregnant and sent us a nice e-mail when Gus was born, a sweet guy. But still, I found it impossible to be the glowing new mom—or even the more plausible exhausted new mom. I wished we were in one of those terrifying talking-baby movies, so Gus could socialize for me. "I'm eight weeks old! I don't sleep very well at night! My mommy is crabby! I already pooped five times today!"

The guy kept trying to lean into the car to sneak a peek, when I suddenly remembered the lesson my high school basketball coach taught me about my ass: "The best way to block out during rebounds is to use your largest muscle!" With my back to him as I fastened the car seat buckles, I shifted my weight from foot to foot, intuiting his moves, and then swinging my hips around to keep him at a distance. I quickly pulled down the sun visor on the car seat, got up some momentum, and reeled around, slamming the door behind me and leaning against it with my arms across my chest.

"Can I take a look?" he said. "I heard he looks a lot like Eli!"

"Nope! No, sorry, no. Sleeping," I said. Gus promptly busted me by screaming, so I panicked and uttered a sentence straight out of some new darkly comical HBO series about an evil cult of celebrity Kabbalah moms. "I'd really love to chat, but I've got to run to my baby massage class! Bye!"

When I arrived at Cheryl's house, she greeted me at the door looking more or less like a 1940s Vargas pinup girl. She was one of those adorable retro girls who never went anywhere without her lipstick on and had an enviable collection of impeccable beaded cashmere sweaters in both pastel and primary colors. Bumping into her on the street was like hearing a bird break into song on a fresh spring morning when you'd just changed your panty liner.

"Hi, you guys!" she said, hugging us as if she had known us all her life. "I can't wait for Gus to meet Daisy!"

I began to relax a little as some stray bits of Catholicism wafted into my psyche. Maybe she was like St. Damien of Molokai, the one who worked with the lepers. St. Cheryl—the patron saint of frazzled moms.

Her apartment, at least what I could see of it so far, was the perfect combination of shiny hardwood floors and gently distressed antiques, the kind of place where every piece of furniture and gleaming tchotchke had a special story behind it. What would someone whose home smelled like a bushel of dewy gardenias—and not like the fetid den of humans on the verge of survival—want with us? Didn't she have better things to do? Here was an attractive woman living the single life in a cute apartment in San Francisco. Why wasn't she sipping a cup of herbal tea in her garden, while wearing a silk slip and nursing a feminine hangover after her illicit Italian lover had returned home to his wife and children? Or at least sleeping in late. Or reading a magazine. Or painting her toenails. Anything.

If I were her, and at this moment I truly wished I were, I would never have invited us into my home. But bless her heart. Unlike many childless women I knew, she actually seemed to really like babies.

"He's gorgeous!" she squealed.

I bit my lip a little and squinted into Gus's eyes. They were enormous and dark, dark blue. As he looked up at me with them, unblinking, drool escaped from the corner of his mouth. I leaned in and wiped it off with the top of my head.

"I feel like an animal," I told Cheryl.

She broke into a huge smile that revealed a set of show-stopping dimples, which went from the top of her cheekbones to her jawline, and said, "Well, that's what we are. We're all animals."

She led us into the living room where she had a tray of pastries and fresh strawberries laid out on a low coffee table. The image of her hopping on her vintage bicycle at the bakery with a pink pastry box tied up with string was almost too much to take. I felt like I had been punched in the gut with the knowledge that I would never again pedal through the streets of a city on a charming old Schwinn with a white basket in front while wearing a flowing skirt and holding a pastry box. Then I realized I'd never done that to begin with, and I felt even worse. I had officially entered that stage of depression where you feel a sense of loss for things you never even had. Bicycles could have meant so much more to me, but now, for the rest of my life, they'd mean nothing but helmets, training wheels, orange flags, and, if I was lucky, a guided retirement tour around Napa Valley with a group of seniors from a suburban community center. Another experience I'd blown. Just as I was settling into a vision of myself on the bike tour, a chatty old biddy with arthritis flare-ups and a neat little helmet of hair, the doorbell rang, thank God, and snapped me out of it.

"It's Baby Doe!" Cheryl cried and went running for the door.

Twice, perhaps even three times, as cute as her name, Baby Doe was the other new mom who would be joining us for the session. She was the leader of a fifteen-member dance troupe called The Devil-Ettes, a spunky D.I.Y. revue that performed synchronized dance routines at nightclubs around town and traveled to rock festivals in Las Vegas and New Orleans. The Devil-Ettes held bake sales, sewed their own sequined costumes, and were beloved as relatively wholesome party girls who didn't take themselves too seriously. Doe's husband was a deejay of exotica music and one of the main honchos in the international Tiki scene, producing a magazine considered the modern bible of Tiki culture. One of the rooms in their house had been turned into a Tiki lounge, complete with a bamboo bar, torches, and straw mats on the floor. Their son's name was Vander Vegas.

If I thought I looked terrible before, the minute Doe walked in with her fresh candy-apple-red dye job done up in little pigtails, I wanted to crawl into a hole. And then I saw what her version of a baby looked like. No zits, no flakes, no stained clothing or waxy ears, just a clean bouncing boy with a sweet disposition who could certainly star in a baby food commercial and fetch a handsome price on the black market.

Cheryl gathered us in the living room and said she wanted to introduce us to someone very special. She had mentioned something about a Daisy, whom I assumed to be her roommate or her cat. She disappeared for a moment, and then brought Daisy out from the bedroom. Daisy was a doll.

"Everybody, this is Miss Daisy!" she said, showing her off around the room, taking care to support her head and neck. She then brought her over for us to admire close up. Daisy had a weathered porcelain face that was heavily lined with a web of superficial cracks, thinning hair, and a pair of jet black eyes that clicked shut when you tilted her head. Daisy was spooky. The boys seemed as unimpressed with her as they were with each other, but Doe and I, being adults trained in the art of social etiquette, tried to match Cheryl's enthusiasm.

"Cute," I said.

"She looks vintage," Baby Doe added.

"She's my little helper," Cheryl said. "Why don't we give them an overview, Daisy? Huh? What do you think?" Daisy nodded her head vigorously, and the demonstration began.

"First we get down on the floor and take off baby's clothes," Cheryl said, carefully removing Daisy's vintage gingham dress, cloth diaper, and lacy ankle socks, folding them neatly on the couch. "We're only going to cover the upper body today."

I looked at Gus's upper body, which was about the size of a hen. This thing would be over in no time, I told myself, as if I were sitting in traffic school. I had already forgotten that this was supposed to be fun and social as well as informational.

After Cheryl showed us the technique, making a peace sign with her fingers and then placing it on her own eyelids to show us how much pressure to use, she invited us to join her on the floor.

The minute I laid Gus down on his cushion, he started screaming. I picked him up and bounced him around, trying to console him as Doe undressed her baby without incident. When Gus settled down a bit, I tried again, but he just screamed some more. He wasn't having it. He was mad. Meanwhile, Vander seemed to be the youngest hedonist in San Francisco. He lolled around, smiling, luxuriating in the warm organic almond oil. He cooed. He gurgled. He looked up at his mommy and practically winked at her.

I checked Gus's diaper. It was dry. I flashed my boob. He didn't want it. He just kept crying, his face getting blotchy and red, his fists thrashing in the air. I looked down into his eyes and tried to rationalize with him. "There will be a day when you realize that you should never, ever turn down a massage when it's offered to you," I told him.

I apologized for ruining the tranquil, classy atmosphere that Cheryl had set up. Gus and I were like those drunk guys who were always stumbling into the public library with their boom boxes and trying to take a piss in the corner.

"It's okay!" Baby Doe said.

"It's fine!" Cheryl said. "It's hard work being a mommy."

"Yeah," I said, straining to be heard over the screams. "I think we'll just go. Thanks anyway! Sorry!"

Instead of getting back in the car, I just keep walking, slipping Gus into this big, smelly fabric pouch around my neck called a sling. Someone had sent me an article that said it would help our bonding as well as provide a convenient hands-free approach to carrying him, and unlike the BabyBjörn, the sling would not adversely affect his hip joints while he was still so young and developing. He loves riding in that thing, all tucked away like an enigma wrapped in a co-nundrum inside a burrito that is covered in crusty stuff. Within seconds he's asleep, so I just keep walking for hours, climbing hill after hill until I reach a vista. I have a picture I keep on my dresser of my parents standing at this same spot. It's from when they first moved out West, and the whole city is spread out below them looking vast and mysterious. Today it looks tiny.

I'm all the way up here, beneath the old steel radio tower, inside the fog, yet I can still pinpoint my first apartment building. I see the park where I used to bring my lunch on sunny days, the eucalyptus grove where I walked my friend's dog, and the club where my old band used to play. Nearly every spot I see triggers some memory—burning my arm at the bakery, picking oranges in the yard of that mansion, and scoring a genie costume from the Russian lady's garage sale. I can't wait for Gus to wake up, so I can show him. Here's where I crashed my car, see? Here's where I bought the greatest vacuum cleaner on earth for ten bucks. Here's where I slept on a roof in a stranger's sleeping bag. And here's where I never dreamed I'd have you.

Acknowledgments

Thanks to my editors Anna Bliss and Bridie Clark; also Kim Hadney, Richard Ljoenes, Kyran Cassidy, Vivian Gomez, Daniel Nayeri, and Paul Olsewski at ReganBooks; Diane Cook at *This American Life*; James Kass at Youth Speaks; Amy Sedaris; and my wonderful agent, Arielle Eckstut at the Levine Greenberg Literary Agency.